MW00881722

Dating the Second Coming of Jesus

Malcolm J. Neelley

Edited by
T. Everett Denton

(author of the book
*Hebrews: From Flawed
to Flawless Fulfilled!*)

Copyright © 2015 by Malcolm J. Neelley.
All rights reserved.

Printed in the United States of America
Printed by CreateSpace, An Amazon.com Company
First Printing, May 2015

ISBN 978-1511692687

Scripture taken from the New King James Version®.
Copyright © 1982 by Thomas Nelson.
Used by permission. All rights reserved.

Books by Malcolm J. Neelley

Proving the Existence of God: A Logical Approach

Dating the Second Coming of Jesus

Contents

Introduction 1

Two Views of the Second Coming 3

Jesus and the Angels 7

The Abomination of Desolation 11

The Great Tribulation 19

The Events after the Tribulation 23

Daniel 12 65

Time Statements 93

Figurative and Idiomatic Language 101

The Firm Belief of the Traditional View 121

Potential Problems from a Firm Belief 123

Reviewing Our Study 125

Living Righteously 131

Introduction

Christians refer to the "Second Coming" as the time when Jesus would return (also called the *parousia,* a Greek word meaning "presence"). It would be the day of judgment, the resurrection of the dead, and the arrival of the new heavens and a new earth.

Most Christians believe that it's not known when the Second Coming would occur, based on two of Jesus' statements: "of that day and hour no one knows, not even the angels of heaven, but My Father only" (Matthew 24:36) and "the Son of Man is coming at an hour you do not expect" (Matthew 24:44). The exact "day and hour" of the Second Coming would not be known, but in this book, we'll see whether the Bible gives any indication for the *approximate* time of the Second Coming by examining the events that would precede it.

Let's begin our study by looking at two viewpoints regarding the Second Coming.

Two Views of the Second Coming

The View of Most Christians

Most Christians believe that the Second Coming—the return of Jesus, the day of judgment, the resurrection of the dead, and the arrival of the new heavens and a new earth—will be literal, visible events: Jesus will physically descend in the clouds, and the dead will physically rise.

Most Christians also believe that, at the end of time, there will be literal, material, cosmic disturbances such as "the heavens will pass away with a great noise, and the elements will melt with fervent heat; both the earth and the works that are in it will be burned up" (2 Peter 3:10); "the moon became like blood," "the stars of heaven fell to the earth," "the sky receded as a scroll when it is rolled up" (Revelation 6:12); and "I saw a new heaven and a new earth, for the first heaven and the first earth had passed away" (Revelation 21:1). Most Christians believe these passages refer to the literal heavenly bodies—planet Earth, our moon, and the stars in the sky—and these heavenly bodies will experience physical cosmic changes when time comes to an end.

The belief is that since Jesus hasn't physically returned, the dead haven't physically risen, and the heavenly bodies haven't experienced those cosmic changes, that means that the Second Coming and the day of judgment cannot have occurred yet.

A Different View of the Second Coming

An increasing number of Christians are taking a closer look at the Bible. They now believe that the passages about the coming of Jesus in the clouds, the resurrection of the dead, and the arrival of the new heavens and a new earth are not referring to literal, physical events; instead, these Christians believe that those passages are using symbolic language to describe the spiritual fulfillment of God's plan: redemption for the faithful and punishment for the ungodly.

Christians who have this alternate view of the Second Coming have a different interpretation of the cosmic disturbances. They believe this language is describing the destruction of the old covenant system, not the destruction of planet Earth and the stars in the sky. They believe the cosmic language is actually covenantal language symbolizing the destruction of Judaism. Those symbolic, covenantal expressions would be seen in passages such as "heaven and earth will pass away" (Mark 13:31); "the heavens will be dissolved, being on fire, and the elements will melt with fervent heat" (2 Peter 3:12); and "the heavens and the earth which are now preserved by the same word, are reserved for fire until the day of judgment and perdition of ungodly men" (2 Peter 3:7).

Christians who believe that Jesus' Second Coming would not be literal and visible might demonstrate how the Bible sometimes uses language that is not meant to be taken literally, such as "the earth melted" in Psalm 46:6: "The nations raged, the kingdoms were moved; He uttered His voice, the earth melted." That passage does not mean that planet Earth literally melted, the same way that 2 Peter 3:10 does not mean that planet Earth would literally "be burned up" where it says "both the earth and the works that are in it will be burned up."

Christians who have this alternate view of the Second Coming believe that since the Bible is using non-literal, symbolic language in passages about the return of Jesus, the day of judgment, the resurrection of the dead, and the arrival of the new heavens and a new earth, that means it's possible that the Second Coming has already occurred. These Christians believe that the Second Coming occurred around the time of the temple's destruction in the first century.

* * * * *

Let's try to determine which viewpoint the Bible more likely supports: whether the events of the Second Coming would be literal and visible, or whether those events would be figurative and symbolic. We'll start by looking at every New Testament passage where Jesus either comes with the angels or sends them.

Jesus and the Angels

Let's examine every New Testament passage where Jesus either comes with the angels (eight passages) or sends them (three passages), or it's implied that He either comes with them or sends them (one passage), where the end result of that passage is the same as those other eleven passages. This total of twelve passages includes two verses—1 Thessalonians 3:13 and Jude 14—where "saints" is probably referring to angels.

Each of these twelve passages depicts the Second Coming, and it's always the same pattern: Jesus either comes with the angels or sends them (either way, it's the same event), and then the day of judgment occurs. This event was to occur after Jesus had died and ascended, so we won't include the following two events involving Jesus and the angels where Jesus had not yet ascended:

- When Jesus was arrested in Matthew 26, He said in verse 53, "Or do you think that I cannot now pray to My Father, and He will provide Me with more than twelve legions of angels?"

- When Jesus first met Nathanael, He said to him in John 1:51, "Most assuredly, I say to you, hereafter you shall see heaven open, and the angels of God ascending and descending upon the Son of Man."

Let's create a table of those twelve "Second Coming" passages where Jesus either comes with the angels or sends them, and then the day of judgment occurs.

Passage	Jesus coming with the angels or sending them	The day of judgment
Matthew 13:41–42	The Son of Man will send out His angels	and they will gather out of His kingdom all things that offend
Matthew 13:49–50	The angels will come forth	[and] separate the wicked from among the just
Matthew 16:27	the Son of Man will come . . . with His angels	and then He will reward each according to his works
Matthew 24:31	He [Jesus] will send His angels	and they will gather together His elect
Matthew 25:31–33	the Son of Man comes in His glory, and all the holy angels with Him	All the nations will be gathered before Him, and He will separate them one from another
Mark 8:38	when He [Jesus] comes . . . with the holy angels	whoever is ashamed of Me and My words in this adulterous and sinful generation, of him the Son of Man also will be ashamed
Mark 13:27	He [Jesus] will send His angels	and gather together His elect
Luke 9:26	when He [Jesus] comes in His own glory . . . and of the holy angels	the Son of Man will be ashamed . . . [of] whoever is ashamed of Me and My words
1 Thessalonians 3:13	at the coming of our Lord Jesus Christ with all His saints	He may establish your hearts blameless in holiness before our God and Father [at the judgment]
2 Thessalonians 1:13	when the Lord Jesus is revealed from heaven with His mighty angels	in flaming fire taking vengeance on those who do not know God, and on those who do not obey the gospel of our Lord Jesus Christ
Jude 14–15	the Lord comes with ten thousands of His saints	to execute judgment on all
Revelation 14:14–19	on the cloud sat One like the Son of Man . . . then another angel came out of the temple which is in heaven	He [Jesus] who sat on the cloud thrust in His sickle on the earth, and the earth was reaped . . . the angel thrust his sickle into the earth and gathered the vine of the earth

In the table, Matthew 24:31 and Mark 13:27 are referring to the day of judgment because their phrase "gather together His elect"—the spiritual harvest/judgment—is equivalent to the gathering/judgment in two other passages: 1) John the Baptist's statement in Matthew 3:12 ("He [Jesus] will . . . gather His wheat into the barn") and 2) Jesus' parable in Matthew 13:47-48 ("a dragnet . . . was cast into the sea . . . and they sat down and gathered the good into vessels").

Also in the table, Mark 8:38 is likely referring to the day of judgment because the "adulterous and sinful generation" of whom Jesus would be ashamed is similar to the "ungodly men" in Jude 4 who would also have shame (and eternal punishment), described in Jude 13 as "raging waves of the sea, foaming up their own shame; wandering stars for whom is reserved the blackness of darkness forever."

As the table shows, every New Testament passage where Jesus either comes with the angels or sends them is always depicting the same event: the Second Coming and the day of judgment. Those twelve passages picture the judgment in various ways, using words such as "gather," "separate," "reward," "ashamed," "vengeance," "judgment," and "reaped."

Two of the "Second Coming" passages in that table—Matthew 24:31 and Mark 13:27—are from the Olivet Discourse. When Jesus sat on the Mount of Olives, He talked to some of His disciples about future events, including the destruction of the temple in Jerusalem and the Second Coming. Most Christians believe that Matthew 24:1–29 or 24:1–35 are about Jerusalem's destruction, and they believe that the remaining verses in Matthew 24 are about the future return of Christ.

In His speech from the Olivet Discourse, Jesus described the events that would lead up to the Second Coming. In the next few chapters, we'll examine those events, starting with the abomination of desolation.

The Abomination of Desolation

In their accounts of the Olivet Discourse, Matthew and Mark instructed their readers to watch for the "abomination of desolation" that was "spoken of by Daniel." Let's compare Luke's account with Matthew's and Mark's to try to identify the abomination of desolation. Here's what Jesus said in each account:

Matthew 24	Mark 13	Luke 21
[15]"Therefore when you see the 'abomination of desolation,' spoken of by Daniel the prophet, standing in the holy place" (whoever reads, let him understand), [16]"then let those who are in Judea flee to the mountains. [17]Let him who is on the housetop not go down to take anything out of his house. [18]And let him who is in the field not go back to get his clothes. [19]But woe to those who are pregnant and to those who are nursing babies in those days! [20]And pray that your flight may not be in winter or on the Sabbath."	[14]"So when you see the 'abomination of desolation,' spoken of by Daniel the prophet, standing where it ought not" (let the reader understand), "then let those who are in Judea flee to the mountains. [15]Let him who is on the housetop not go down into the house, nor enter to take anything out of his house. [16]And let him who is in the field not go back to get his clothes. [17]But woe to those who are pregnant and to those who are nursing babies in those days! [18]And pray that your flight may not be in winter."	[20]"But when you see Jerusalem surrounded by armies, then know that its desolation is near. [21]Then let those who are in Judea flee to the mountains, let those who are in the midst of her depart, and let not those who are in the country enter her. [22]For these are the days of vengeance, that all things which are written may be fulfilled. [23a]But woe to those who are pregnant and to those who are nursing babies in those days!"

In Matthew 24 in the table above, the people were instructed to flee when they saw the abomination of desolation "standing in the holy place."

In the last part of Mark 13:14, those same people were instructed to flee when they saw the abomination of desolation "standing where it ought not."

In Luke 21:21, those same people were instructed to flee "when you see Jerusalem surrounded by armies."

In all three passages, the same people were instructed to flee when they saw a specific event. That means:

the specific event in Matthew = the specific event in Mark = the specific event in Luke

Therefore,

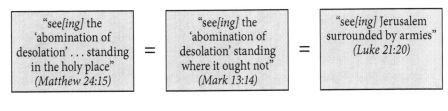

which means:

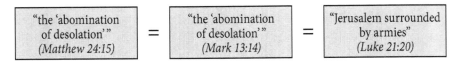

As the above chart shows, the abomination of desolation was equivalent to the armies that surrounded Jerusalem.

Another reason why those verses from Matthew, Mark, and Luke are equivalent is because they share the same Greek word for "desolation"—*eremosis*:

Matthew 24:15	when you see the abomination of	**desolation**	. . . standing in the holy place
Mark 13:14	when you see the abomination of	**desolation**	. . . standing where it ought not
Luke 21:20	when you see Jerusalem surrounded by armies, then know that its	**desolation**	is near

The armies that surrounded Jerusalem were the "abomination of desolation":

- They were the "abomination" because they were standing on holy ground; they were "standing in the holy place" and "standing where it ought not."

- Those armies caused "desolation," fulfilling Jesus' prophecy in Matthew 23:37–38: "O Jerusalem, Jerusalem, the one who kills the prophets and stones those who are sent to her! . . . Your house is left to you desolate."

Eusebius, an early church historian who lived from about A.D. 263–339, wrote that "the people of the church in Jerusalem had been commanded by a revelation, vouchsafed to approved men there before the war, to leave the city and to dwell in a certain town of Perea called Pella" (*Ecclesiastical History*, book 3, chapter 5, section 3).

The abomination of desolation and the escape from Judea have already occurred—in the first century.

Based on what we've determined so far, let's create a chart that sequences the prophecies from the Olivet Discourse. That chart (and most of the ones that follow) will contain boxed text arranged in columns (vertical) and rows (horizontal). The columns will show the flow of verses from a specific book of the Bible, and the rows—when an equal sign is used between the boxed text—will show parallel verses. Beneath the rows, there will sometimes be a horizontal brace with a notation, such as the time period for a prophecy's fulfillment.

| "Therefore when you see the 'abomination of desolation,' spoken of by Daniel the prophet, standing in the holy place" (whoever reads, let him understand), *(Matthew 24:15)* | = | "So when you see the 'abomination of desolation,' spoken of by Daniel the prophet, standing where it ought not" (let the reader understand), *(Mark 13:14)* | = | "But when you see Jerusalem surrounded by armies, then know that its desolation is near." *(Luke 21:20)* |

Time period for the prophecy's fulfillment: the first century

| "then" *(Matthew 24:16)* | = | "then" *(Mark 13:14)* | = | "Then" *(Luke 21:21)* |

Time period for the fulfillment: still the first century

| "let those who are in Judea flee to the mountains. Let him who is on the housetop not go down to take anything out of his house. And let him who is in the field not go back to get his clothes. But woe to those who are pregnant and to those who are nursing babies in those days! And pray that your flight may not be in winter or on the Sabbath." *(Matthew 24:16–20)* | = | "let those who are in Judea flee to the mountains. Let him who is on the housetop not go down into the house, nor enter to take anything out of his house. And let him who is in the field not go back to get his clothes. But woe to those who are pregnant and to those who are nursing babies in those days! And pray that your flight may not be in winter." *(Mark 13:14–18)* | = | "let those who are in Judea flee to the mountains, let those who are in the midst of her depart, and let not those who are in the country enter her. For these are the days of vengeance, that all things which are written may be fulfilled. But woe to those who are pregnant and to those who are nursing babies in those days!" *(Luke 21:21–23)* |

Time period for the fulfillment: still the first century

In the table at the beginning of this chapter, Jesus said in Luke 21:22, "For these are the days of vengeance, that all things which are written may be fulfilled." Let's look at that statement in the context of Luke 21:20–24:

> ²⁰"But when you see Jerusalem surrounded by armies, then know that its desolation is near. ²¹Then let those who are in Judea flee to the mountains, let those who are in the midst of her depart, and let not those who are in the country enter her. ²²**For these are the days of vengeance, that all things which are written may be fulfilled.** ²³But woe to those who are pregnant and to those who are nursing babies in those days! For there will be great distress in the land and wrath upon this people. ²⁴And they will fall by the edge of the sword, and be led away captive into all nations. And Jerusalem will be trampled by Gentiles until the times of the Gentiles are fulfilled."

In verse 20, Jesus prophesied that Jerusalem would be surrounded by armies, and in verse 22, He described that time as "the days of vengeance." Jesus was prophesying about the first-century Roman tribulation of the Jews ("the days of vengeance"). Those first-century "days of vengeance" would fulfill Jesus' prophecy from Matthew 23 and Luke 11 (with emphasis added to show that the first-century "days of vengeance" would occur in the first-century's "this generation"):

" 'Therefore, indeed, I send you prophets, wise men, and scribes: some of them you will kill and crucify, and some of them you will scourge in your synagogues and persecute from city to city, that on you may come all the righteous blood shed on the earth, from the blood of righteous Abel to the blood of Zechariah, son of Berechiah, whom you murdered between the temple and the altar. Assuredly, I say to you, all these things will come upon **this generation**.' " *(Matthew 23:34–36)*	=	"Therefore the wisdom of God also said, 'I will send them prophets and apostles, and some of them they will kill and persecute,' that the blood of all the prophets which was shed from the foundation of the world may be required of **this generation**, from the blood of Abel to the blood of Zechariah who perished between the altar and the temple. Yes, I say to you, it shall be required of **this generation**." *(Luke 11:49–51)*

Also 21:32

In Acts 7, when Stephen spoke before the council of the Jews, he echoed some of Jesus' words from the chart above:

> [51]"You stiff-necked and uncircumcised in heart and ears! You always resist the Holy Spirit; as your fathers did, so do you. [52]Which of the prophets did your fathers not persecute? And they killed those who foretold the coming of the Just One, of whom you now have become the betrayers and murderers, [53]who have received the law by the direction of angels and have not kept it."

In 2 Thessalonians 1:6, Paul also referred to those first-century "days of vengeance" of the Jews, where he wrote that "it is a righteous thing with God to repay with tribulation those who trouble you." Those first-century Christians were troubled by the first-century Jews, so the "great tribulation" (Matthew 24:21) and "the days of vengeance" occurred in the first century.

In the next chapter, we'll examine the great tribulation, which was the next event that would occur before the Second Coming.

The Great Tribulation

Let's look at the next set of verses from the Olivet Discourse to see whether they, too, are referring to first-century events.

Matthew 24	Mark 13	Luke 21
²¹"For <u>then</u> there will be great <u>tribulati</u>on, such as has not been since the beginning of the world until this time, no, nor ever shall be. ²²And unless those days were shortened, no flesh would be saved; but for the elect's sake those days will be shortened."	¹⁹"For in <u>those days</u> there will be <u>tribulati</u>on, such as has not been since the beginning of the creation which God created until this time, nor ever shall be. ²⁰And unless the Lord had shortened those days, no flesh would be saved; but for the elect's sake, whom He chose, He shortened the days."	²³ᵇ"For there will be great <u>distress</u> in the land and wrath upon this people. ²⁴And they will fall by the edge of the sword, and be led away captive into all nations. And Jerusalem will be trampled by Gentiles until the times of the Gentiles are fulfilled."

In the above three accounts, we see that there would be "great tribulation" (Matthew), "tribulation" (Mark), and "great distress" (Luke), and we also see when that tribulation would occur. In Matthew 24:21, we see the time statement "then," and in Mark 13:19 we see "in those days." The previous verses—the abomination of desolation and the escape from Judea—were first-century events, so the tribulation that would occur "then" and "in those days" was also a first-century event.

Joseph Henry Thayer (1828–1901), a U.S. Bible scholar and renowned lexicographer who compiled a Greek-English dictionary of the New Testament, described the Greek word for "tribulation" as "oppression, affliction, tribulation, distress, straits" and, specifically in Matthew 24 and Mark 13, Thayer described "tribulation" as "of the afflictions of those hard pressed by siege and the calamities of war."

Some Christians might argue that the "tribulation" and "distress" from the Olivet Discourse is not referring to a first-century event. They would refer to Matthew's description of that tribulation: "such as has not been since the beginning of the world until this time, no, nor ever shall be." These Christians might say that the tribulation in World War II, for example, was greater than the first-century tribulation of the Jews; therefore, they would argue that the world's greatest "tribulation" could not have occurred in the first century. We need to recognize, however, that the tribulation from the Olivet Discourse actually is referring to a first-century event. We have demonstrated that the abomination of desolation and the escape from Judea were first-century events, so the tribulation—the event that would occur "then" and "in those days"—would also be a first-century event. We learned earlier that the first-century "days of vengeance" (Luke 21:22) was equivalent to the first-century "great tribulation" (Matthew 24:21).

Why did Jesus describe that first-century tribulation as "such as has not been since the beginning of the world until this time, no, nor ever shall be"? It's because the fall of Jerusalem was the worst devastation that the Old Covenant "world" had ever experienced—or ever would, since it would be their last devastation. It was the worst devastation of the Old Covenant world not only because of the number of people who died; it was also the worst because it was the total destruction of Judaism. Annihilation is the worst that can happen.

On the next page, let's add to our chart the time statements from Matthew 24:21 and Mark 13:19, followed by the prophecy of the tribulation. To keep the chart on one page, we'll present just the key points from the previous full-page chart.

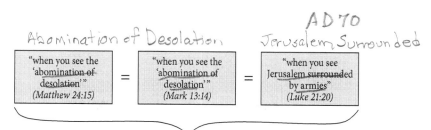

Abomination of Desolation

AD 70
Jerusalem Surrounded

| "when you see the 'abomination of desolation'" (Matthew 24:15) | = | "when you see the 'abomination of desolation'" (Mark 13:14) | = | "when you see Jerusalem surrounded by armies" (Luke 21:20) |

Time period for the prophecy's fulfillment: the first century

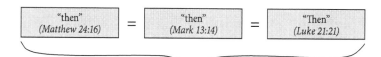

| "then" (Matthew 24:16) | = | "then" (Mark 13:14) | = | "Then" (Luke 21:21) |

Time period for the fulfillment: still the first century

Flee

| "let those who are in Judea flee to the mountains" (Matthew 24:16) | = | "let those who are in Judea flee to the mountains" (Mark 13:14) | = | "let those who are in Judea flee to the mountains" (Luke 21:21) |

Time period for the fulfillment: still the first century

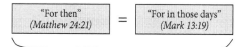

| "For then" (Matthew 24:21) | = | "For in those days" (Mark 13:19) |

Time period for the fulfillment: still the first century

Great Tribulation

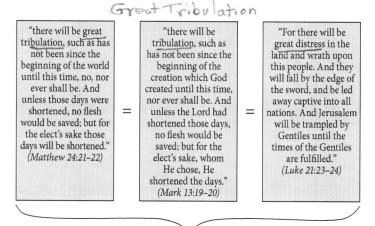

| "there will be great tribulation, such as has not been since the beginning of the world until this time, no, nor ever shall be. And unless those days were shortened, no flesh would be saved; but for the elect's sake those days will be shortened." (Matthew 24:21–22) | = | "there will be tribulation, such as has not been since the beginning of the creation which God created until this time, nor ever shall be. And unless the Lord had shortened those days, no flesh would be saved; but for the elect's sake, whom He chose, He shortened the days." (Mark 13:19–20) | = | "For there will be great distress in the land and wrath upon this people. And they will fall by the edge of the sword, and be led away captive into all nations. And Jerusalem will be trampled by Gentiles until the times of the Gentiles are fulfilled." (Luke 21:23–24) |

Time period for the fulfillment: still the first century

* * * * *

Before we continue our examination of the Olivet Discourse, it should be noted that Matthew 24 isn't perfectly chronological. Jesus will present a point, then back up a little, move up to another point, back up again, then move up again. For example, in verses 5–14 (in which He spoke of certain aspects of the end times), He ends with "then the end will come." Then, in verses 15–22, He spoke of other things which would occur within the time frame before "the end" of verse 14. Next, in verses 23–28, He spoke of yet other incidents which would occur within the time frame before "the end." Then, "the end" is described in verses 29–31. Next, in verses 32 and following, Jesus cautions His own people against any laziness or unconcern regarding that time, which continues right into Matthew 25. Jesus was telling His disciples that they needed to be gone before the armies tightened up around Jerusalem.

In the next chapter, we'll look at the events that occurred after the first-century tribulation.

The Events after the Tribulation

Since Matthew 24 is not chronological, let's move ahead to Matthew 24:29–31 and the parallel in Mark 13:24–27 where Jesus resumes His discussion about the tribulation "of those days" in the first century. Matthew and Mark describe the events that would happen after the tribulation. We want to be sure those events happened after the tribulation, so we'll omit Luke's account because he doesn't give the time statement "after the tribulation" or "after that tribulation."

Matthew 24	Mark 13
[29]"Immediately after the tribulation of those days the sun will be darkened, and the moon will not give its light; the stars will fall from heaven, and the powers of the heavens will be shaken. [30]Then the sign of the Son of Man will appear in heaven, and then all the tribes of the earth will mourn,"	[24]"But in those days, after that tribulation, the sun will be darkened, and the moon will not give its light; [25]the stars of heaven will fall, and the powers in the heavens will be shaken."

The tribulation "of those days" and "in those days" in the above passages is the same first-century tribulation as the one "in those days" (Mark 13:24) and "then" (Matthew 24:29). In the above passages, Matthew and Mark discuss some of the events that would occur after the tribulation; therefore, those events—like the tribulation—were to occur in the first century.

In Matthew 24:29 and Mark 13:24–25 in the table above, we see some of those first-century events:

- the sun will be darkened
- the moon will not give its light
- the stars will fall from heaven
- the powers of the heavens will be shaken

It can be demonstrated that those are figurative expressions:

1. Those prophecies were fulfilled in the first century, but since there's no first-century record that the heavenly bodies experienced physical cosmic changes, that means that the Bible is using figurative and symbolic language in those passages.

   This particular type of language is called apocalyptic language, where dramatic and frightening images, such as cosmic destruction, are used to express in human terms the judgment and awesome power of God. Apocalyptic language is used to dramatically describe the destruction of any given people's world—the downfall of a dynasty, the capture of a city, or the overthrow of a nation. The above four bulleted prophecies from the Olivet Discourse are referring to the destruction of the first-century Jewish world (Judaism), not the destruction of the sun, our moon, the stars in the sky, or heaven.

2. In Isaiah 13, there's a prophecy about God's judgment against Babylon (which was conquered by Cyrus the Great of Persia in 539 B.C.). That prophecy contains the same kind of figurative, apocalyptic language that we saw in the above four bulleted prophecies from the Olivet Discourse. Let's compare Isaiah's wording with Matthew's and Mark's:

For the stars of heaven and their constellations will not give their light; the sun will be darkened in its going forth, and the moon will not cause its light to shine. . . . "I will shake the heavens, and the earth will move out of her place, in the wrath of the Lord of hosts and in the day of His fierce anger." *(Isaiah 13:10 and 13)*	"the sun will be darkened, and the moon will not give its light; the stars will fall from heaven, and the powers of the heavens will be shaken. Then the sign of the Son of Man will appear in heaven, and then all the tribes of the earth will mourn," *(Matthew 24:29–30)*	"the sun will be darkened, and the moon will not give its light; the stars of heaven will fall, and the powers in the heavens will be shaken." *(Mark 13:24–25)*

God's prophecy in Isaiah 13 above was fulfilled when Babylon was conquered in the days of the Old Testament, but since those cosmic events did not occur literally, that means that Isaiah was using figurative language.

In the above passages, both Isaiah and Jesus were addressing a Hebrew audience, using identical symbolic language that their Hebrew audience would understand. Since the language in Isaiah was figurative, the language in Matthew and Mark would also be figurative, unless there's a reason to believe that God (the Bible's Author) wanted it understood in a different way. Matthew and Mark—like Isaiah—were using figurative language to depict the mighty power of God and the judgment of His disobedient people.

Let's look again at the table we had created at the beginning of this chapter. We'll then compare those passages to Acts 2 and Joel 2-3 to verify that the prophecies in that table were to be fulfilled in the first century.

Matthew 24	Mark 13
29"Immediately after the tribulation of those days the sun will be darkened, and the moon will not give its light; the stars will fall from heaven, and the powers of the heavens will be shaken. 30Then the sign of the Son of Man will appear in heaven, and then all the tribes of the earth will mourn,"	24"But in those days, after that tribulation, the sun will be darkened, and the moon will not give its light; 25the stars of heaven will fall, and the powers in the heavens will be shaken."

In Acts 2, the Jewish audience had witnessed the disciples' miraculous ability to speak in tongues. Peter said in verse 16 that **"this is that** which was spoken by the prophet Joel" *[King James Version; emphasis added]*. Peter was testifying that the prophecies from Joel 2 were now starting to be fulfilled—at that time, "in the last days *[the last days of the Mosaic age]*" (Acts 2:17). In Acts 2:19–20, Peter quoted one of the prophecies from Joel 2:

> "I *[God]* will show wonders in heaven above and signs in the earth beneath: blood and fire and vapor of smoke. The sun shall be turned into darkness, and the moon into blood, before the coming of the great and awesome day of the Lord."

That prophecy parallels the prophecies from Matthew 24 and Mark 13 in the table above. We had demonstrated that those apocalyptic prophecies from the Olivet Discourse were fulfilled in the first century, and Peter verified that fact when he testified that Joel's apocalyptic prophecies—the same prophecies as in Matthew and Mark—would be fulfilled in the first century ("in the last days"). Joel 3, which is a prophecy about Jerusalem's demise, also verifies that Joel 2 was prophesying about first-century events.

In that table above, the prophecy in Matthew 24:30a says, "Then the sign of the Son of Man will appear in heaven, and then all the tribes of the earth will mourn. . . ." That verse is a continuation of the Olivet Discourse prophecies that were to be fulfilled in the first century. In the days of the great tribulation, the people did not *literally* see Jesus; instead, they saw the *signs* of Him. When they witnessed the fulfillment of Jesus' prophecies—such as the destruction of the temple—they would have recognized, or "seen," the hand of God as the architect behind those events. When the Jewish nation—"the tribes of the earth"—saw "the sign of the Son of Man," that means that they saw the evidence of Jesus in those fulfilled prophecies. They would "mourn" because they had rejected Jesus; they realized—too late—that Jesus was the Messiah. They recognized that Jesus' prophecy about them had been fulfilled: "'I [God] will send them prophets and apostles, and some of them they will kill and persecute,' that the blood of all the prophets which was shed from the foundation of the world may be required of **this generation**" (Luke 11:49–50; emphasis added).

On the next page, let's add to our chart the Olivet Discourse verses that appeared at the beginning of this chapter. As we did before, we'll keep the chart on one page by presenting just the key points from the previous Olivet Discourse chart.

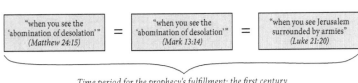

Time period for the prophecy's fulfillment: the first century

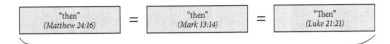

Time period for the fulfillment: still the first century

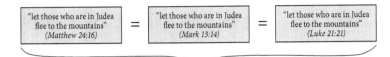

Time period for the fulfillment: still the first century

Time period for the fulfillment: still the first century

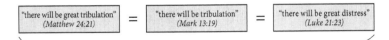

Time period for the fulfillment: still the first century

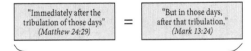

Time period for the fulfillment: still the first century

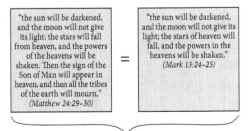

Time period for the fulfillment: still the first century

All of the Olivet Discourse prophecies that we've examined so far were to be fulfilled in the first century. Let's look at the next set of prophecies from Matthew and Mark, which is a continuation of the prophecies that were to be fulfilled in the first century.

Matthew 24	Mark 13
[30]"and they will see the Son of Man coming on the clouds of heaven with power and great glory. [31]And He will send His angels with a great sound of a trumpet, and they will gather together His elect from the four winds, from one end of heaven to the other."	[26]"Then they will see the Son of Man coming in the clouds with great power and glory. [27]And then He will send His angels, and gather together His elect from the four winds, from the farthest part of earth to the farthest part of heaven."

In the accounts from Matthew and Mark above, Jesus prophesied that He would be seen coming on/in the clouds. This prophecy was to be fulfilled in the first century after the tribulation, but since there's no first-century record that Jesus was literally seen coming on or in literal clouds, that means that Jesus was using figurative language. We'll examine that type of language later in this book.

Matthew 24:31 (above) says, "And He [Jesus] will send His angels with a great sound of a trumpet, and they will gather together His elect from the four winds, from one end of heaven to the other." The parallel verse in Mark 13:27 (above) says, "And then He will send His angels, and gather together His elect from the four winds, from the farthest part of earth to the farthest part of heaven."

Those passages from Matthew and Mark are significant for two reasons:

1. They are two of the twelve "Second Coming" passages that we had listed earlier. Those passages from Matthew and Mark are a prophecy about the Second Coming and the day of judgment. We had mentioned that those two passages

were referring to the day of judgment because the gathering (the spiritual harvest) in those verses is equivalent to the gathering/judgment in Matthew 3:12 and 13:47–48. Let's compare those passages from Matthew 3 and 13 with the two passages from the Olivet Discourse:

Matthew 3:12	He *[Jesus]* will . . .	**gather**	His wheat into the barn
Matthew 13:47–48	a dragnet . . . was cast into the sea . . . and they sat down and	**gathered**	the good into vessels
Matthew 24:31	they *[Jesus' angels]* will	**gather**	together His elect
Mark 13:27	*[Jesus will]*	**gather**	together His elect

2. That "Second Coming" prophecy from Matthew 24 and Mark 13 is a continuation of the Olivet Discourse prophecies that were to be fulfilled in the first century. Therefore, the "Second Coming" prophecy from Matthew and Mark would also be fulfilled in the first century.

We see, then, that in the Olivet Discourse, Jesus prophesied that the events of the Second Coming would occur in the first century: they would see the Son of Man coming on the clouds, He would send His angels with the sound of a trumpet, and the angels would gather together His elect.

In the following chart, we can see that Jesus verified that the Second Coming would occur in that first-century generation.

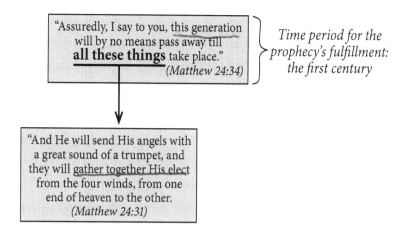

In the chart above, the phrase "all these things" from Matthew 24:34 refers back to Matthew 24:31 (indicated by the arrow in the chart), where we see the prophecy of the Second Coming. In that chart, Jesus was indicating that the Second Coming (verse 31) would be one of the events that would occur in that first-century generation (verse 34).

In Matthew 24:31 in the chart, the fact that the harvest would occur in the first century was confirmed by Jesus in Matthew 13:39–42, where He explained the parable of the tares (weeds) to His disciples:

> "The enemy who sowed them is the devil, the harvest is the end of the age, and the reapers are the angels. Therefore as the tares are gathered and burned in the fire, so it will be at the end of this age. The Son of Man will send out His angels, and they will gather out of His kingdom all things that offend, and those who practice lawlessness, and will cast them into the furnace of fire. There will be wailing and gnashing of teeth."

Mt 13:39-42

In the passage above, the "harvest" was part of the "gather*[ing]* together *[of]* His elect" from Matthew 24:31 in the chart. Both passages are referring to the spiritual harvest/Second Coming. Jesus explained that the harvest/gathering of the tares was to occur "at the end of **this** age" (emphasis added). Jesus was living in the Mosaic age, so the harvest/Second Coming was to occur "at the end of *[the Mosaic]* age." As we'll see in more detail later, the Mosaic age ended at the time of Jerusalem's destruction, when God destroyed Judaism—the temple, the Levitical priesthood, and the sacrificial system—by means of the first-century tribulation by the Roman armies.

Since Jesus was prophesying that the harvest/Second Coming would occur at the end of the Mosaic age, and since the end of the Mosaic age would occur at the time of Jerusalem's destruction, that means that the harvest/Second Coming was to occur at the time of Jerusalem's destruction.

When we further examine that "end of this age" time statement, we find additional proof that the Second Coming was to occur in the first century. In His explanation of the parable of the tares, Jesus said,

> "Therefore as the tares are gathered and burned in the fire, so it will be at the end of this age. The Son of Man will send out His angels, and they will gather out of His kingdom all things that offend, and those who practice lawlessness, and will cast them into the furnace of fire."

Those two sentences are parallel: the tares would be "gathered and burned in the fire" (the first sentence), and the unrighteous would be "gather*[ed]*" and "cast . . . into the furnace of fire" (the second sentence). Since those two sentences are parallel, and since "the tares *[would be]* gathered and burned . . . at the end of *[the Mosaic]* age" in the first century, that means that "the Son of Man *[would]* send out His angels" to "cast *[the unrighteous]* into the furnace of fire" at the end of the Mosaic age in the first century. Since those are prophecies of the final judgment/Second Coming, and since those prophecies were to occur at the end of the Mosaic age in the first century, that means that the final judgment/Second Coming was to occur at the end of the Mosaic age in the first century.

Therefore, the first-century timing of the Second Coming was prophesied by Jesus in His parable of the tares, and that first-century timing was also prophesied by Jesus in His Olivet Discourse (shown in the chart above).

The Second Coming occurred in the first century, but it was not a literal, bodily return of Jesus. (We'll later study the nature of the Second Coming.)

Most Christians believe that this Olivet Discourse prophecy was not about the *actual* Second Coming; they believe this prophecy was referring to *a* coming of Jesus, not *the* Second Coming. They believe that those verses from Matthew and Mark are just a *picture* of the second/last coming. Most Christians believe that Matthew 24:1–29 or 24:1–35 are about Jerusalem's destruction, so, since Jesus did not return bodily at that time, they believe that Jesus was not prophesying about the actual Second Coming in Matthew 24:31 ("And He will send His angels with a great sound of a trumpet, and they will gather together His elect from the four winds, from one end of heaven to the other.").

Jesus *was* prophesying, however, about the actual Second Coming, and was not prophesying about a picture of it. There's no indication in the Olivet Discourse text that Jesus was prophesying about a picture of the Second Coming. Matthew 24:31 shows that after the end of the first-century tribulation, Jesus "will send His angels with a great sound of a trumpet, and they will gather together His elect from the four winds, from one end of heaven to the other." Those are the *actual events* of the Second Coming—Jesus sending His angels, the trumpet, and the spiritual harvest of the faithful. This is one of the Second Coming verses listed earlier in this book, and, like those other verses, it's describing the *actual* Second Coming, and not a *picture* of it. The *actual* Second Coming occurred in the first century after the great tribulation, but it was not a literal, bodily return of Jesus.

Another reason why Jesus was prophesying about the actual Second Coming—and not a picture of it—is because all remaining prophecy from the Old Testament was fulfilled no later than around A.D. 70. This will be demonstrated later in this chapter.

* * * * *

Earlier in this book, we looked at Jesus' statement in Luke 21:22: "For these are the days of vengeance, that all things which are written may be fulfilled." We demonstrated that "the days of vengeance" was equivalent to the first-century Roman tribulation of the Jews. The fact that "the days of vengeance" occurred in the first century is significant.

Let's start by looking at Luke 21:22 again, but let's focus on the last part of that statement: "For these are the days of vengeance, that all things which are written may be fulfilled." At the time Jesus delivered His Olivet Discourse, "all things which are written" would have been the prophecies from the Old Testament—the Law and the Prophets. In that verse from Luke, Jesus was prophesying that in "the days of vengeance"—in the first-century days of the great tribulation—all remaining prophecy from the Old Testament would be fulfilled so that "all things which are written may be fulfilled." The Old Testament prophecies that had not yet been fulfilled—but *would be fulfilled* in the "days of vengeance" in the first century—included the Second Coming, the day of judgment, the resurrection of the dead, the passing away the first heaven and the first earth, and the arrival of a new heaven and a new earth. Those prophecies can be seen in the following Old Testament passages:

Prophecy of the Second Coming

"I was watching in the night visions, and behold, One like the Son of Man, coming with the clouds of heaven! He came to the Ancient of Days, and they brought Him near before Him. Then to Him was given dominion and glory and a kingdom, that all peoples, nations, and languages should serve Him. His dominion is an everlasting dominion, which shall not pass away, and His kingdom the one which shall not be destroyed. . . . 'the saints of the Most High shall receive the kingdom, and possess the kingdom forever, even forever and ever.'" (Daniel 7:13–14 and 18)

Prophecies of the opening of the Book of Life and the resurrection of the dead

". . . And at that time your people shall be delivered, every one who is found written in the book. And many of those who sleep in the dust of the earth shall awake, some to everlasting life, some to shame and everlasting contempt. Those who are wise shall shine like the brightness of the firmament, and those who turn many to righteousness like the stars forever and ever." (Daniel 12:1–3)

Prophecies of the passing away of the first heaven and the first earth and the arrival of a new heaven and a new earth

"Lift up your eyes to the heavens, and look on the earth beneath. For the heavens will vanish away like smoke, the earth will grow old like a garment, and those who dwell in it will die in like manner; but My salvation will be forever, and My righteousness will not be abolished. . . . For behold, I create new heavens and a new earth; and the former shall not be remembered or come to mind." (Isaiah 51:6, 65:17)

Those Old Testament prophecies were prophecies about the actual events; they weren't prophecies about *pictures* of the events. For example, in the above passages from Daniel 12:1–3, there's no indication that these are pictures of the events; those prophecies are about the actual event of the opening of the Book of Life, the actual event of the resurrection of the dead, and the actual event of the final judgment of the dead. Those actual events were fulfilled in the first century along with the rest of the remaining Old Testament prophecies. Let's create a logical sequence that demonstrates the first-century fulfillment of those prophecies from Daniel:

1. The passing away of heaven and earth is closely connected to the day of judgment and the Second Coming.

2. The passing away of heaven and earth is equivalent to the destruction of Judaism.

3. Therefore, the destruction of Judaism is closely connected to the day of judgment and the Second Coming.

4. Since the destruction of Judaism is closely connected to the day of judgment and the Second Coming, and since the destruction of Judaism occurred in the first century, that means that the day of judgment and the Second Coming occurred in the first century.

Those Old Testament prophecies were fulfilled in the first-century days of the great tribulation, but since Jesus did not return bodily, all of the dead did not physically rise from their graves, and the first heaven and the first planet Earth were not literally replaced with a new heaven and new planet Earth, those events were not literal. The fact that those events occurred, but were not literal, visible events, forces a figurative interpretation. Even if a person doesn't understand how those events could be figurative, it's *still* a fact that they *were* figurative because those events *did* occur in the first century, but since there's no record that those events occurred literally and visibly, it necessitates a figurative interpretation. Those passages are using symbolic language to describe the spiritual fulfillment of God's plan: redemption for the faithful and punishment for the ungodly. We'll examine this figurative, symbolic language later in this book.

Let's look again at Jesus' statement in Luke 21:22: "For these are the days of vengeance, that all things which are written may be fulfilled." Earlier, we demonstrated the meaning of that statement: in the first century (in "the days of vengeance"), all remaining prophecy from the Old Testament would be fulfilled ("all things which are written may be fulfilled"). Since all remaining prophecy from the Old Testament was fulfilled in the days of the great tribulation ("the days of vengeance"), that means that the Second Coming—one of those remaining prophecies—was fulfilled in the first century. Let's try to find additional passages that show that same pattern: where the great tribulation occurs, followed by the events of the Second Coming.

Let's create a table, starting with Luke 21:22. The verses will be paraphrased in the second and third column heads, which say, "In the first-century days of the great tribulation . . . all remaining prophecy from the Old Testament will be fulfilled—including the events of the Second Coming."

Verse	In the first-century days of the great tribulation . . .	all remaining prophecy from the Old Testament will be fulfilled— including the events of the Second Coming.
Luke 21:22	"For these are the days of vengeance,	that all things which are written may be fulfilled."

In our study of the Olivet Discourse earlier in this chapter, we saw that the prophecy of the great tribulation was followed by the prophecy of the events of the Second Coming. Let's add those passages from Matthew and Luke to our table:

Verse	In the first-century days of the great tribulation . . .	all remaining prophecy from the Old Testament will be fulfilled— including the events of the Second Coming.
Luke 21:22	"For these are the days of vengeance,	that all things which are written may be fulfilled."
Matthew 24:21, 31	"For then there will be great tribulation . . .	And He will send His angels with a great sound of a trumpet, and they will gather together His elect from the four winds, from one end of heaven to the other."
Mark 13:19, 27	"For in those days there will be tribulation . . .	And then He will send His angels, and gather together His elect from the four winds, from the farthest part of earth to the farthest part of heaven."

In the verse from Luke in the table above, Jesus presented a general truth; in Matthew and Mark, He presented examples that *demonstrated* that truth. In Luke, Jesus prophesied that all remaining prophecy from the Old Testament would be fulfilled in the days of the great tribulation; in Matthew and Mark, He prophesied that the Second Coming—one of those remaining prophecies—would be fulfilled at that time. Since all remaining prophecy from the Old Testament would be fulfilled in the days of the first-century tribulation, and since the Second Coming was one of those remaining prophecies, the *actual* Second Coming—and not a *picture* of it—*had to occur* in the first century. If the Second Coming *didn't* occur in the first century, then Jesus was mistaken when He said that "**all things** which are written may be fulfilled" in "the days of vengeance *[in the days of the first-century tribulation]*" *[emphasis added]*.

Let's look again at Jesus' statement in Luke 21:22: "For these are the days of vengeance, that all things which are written may be fulfilled." In verse 32 of that same chapter of Luke, Jesus emphasized the fact that all remaining prophecy would be fulfilled in the first century when He said, "Assuredly, I say to you, **this generation** will by no means pass away till all things take place" *[emphasis added]*. The phrase "all things" refers to *all* of the remaining prophecies from the Scriptures. In that verse 32, Jesus was saying that all remaining prophecy from the Scriptures would be fulfilled within that first-century generation.

Let's create a table to show that parallel between Luke 21:22 and 32. Those two verses will be paraphrased in the second and third column heads, which say, "In the first century . . . all remaining prophecy from the Old Testament will be fulfilled."

Verse	In the first century . . .	all remaining prophecy from the Old Testament will be fulfilled.
Luke 21:22	"For these are the days of vengeance,	that all things which are written may be fulfilled."
Luke 21:32	"Assuredly, I say to you, this generation will by no means pass away	till all things take place."

The Second Coming was one of the prophecies from the Old Testament, and since all remaining prophecy from the Old Testament would be fulfilled in "the days of vengeance" (in the first century), that means that the Second Coming occurred in the first century. This shows that Jesus was prophesying about the *actual* Second Coming— not a *picture* of it—in the Olivet Discourse in Matthew 24:31 and Mark 13:27.

Jesus could not have been prophesying about a *picture* of the Second Coming because He'd be contradicting Himself; He'd be saying that all remaining prophecy would be fulfilled in the first century, but He'd also be saying that all remaining prophecy would *not* be fulfilled in the first century because (supposedly) the prophecy of the *actual* Second Coming would not be fulfilled then.

* * * * *

We have now demonstrated that the remaining Old Testament prophecies were fulfilled in the first century, but most Christians would still believe that the Second Coming events in Revelation have not yet been fulfilled.

We can find parallels between the prophecies in Revelation and the three Old Testament prophecies that we listed earlier (the indented list in the small type with the italic headings). Let's create a chart that shows those parallels, and then let's evaluate those parallels.

"I was watching in the night visions, and behold, One like the Son of Man, coming with the clouds of heaven! He came to the Ancient of Days, and they brought Him near before Him. Then to Him was given dominion and glory and a kingdom, that all peoples, nations, and languages should serve Him. His dominion is an everlasting dominion, which shall not pass away, and His kingdom the one which shall not be destroyed. . . . 'the saints of the Most High shall receive the kingdom, and possess the kingdom forever, even forever and ever.'"
(Daniel 7:13–14, 18)

=

Then I *[the apostle John]* looked, and behold, a white cloud, and on the cloud sat One like the Son of Man, having on His head a golden crown, and in His hand a sharp sickle. And another angel came out of the temple, crying with a loud voice to Him who sat on the cloud, "Thrust in Your sickle and reap, for the time has come for You to reap, for the harvest of the earth is ripe." So He who sat on the cloud thrust in His sickle on the earth, and the earth was reaped. . . . So the angel thrust his sickle into the earth and gathered the vine of the earth, and threw it into the great winepress of the wrath of God.
(Revelation 14:14–16, 19)

Prophecies of the Second Coming and the day of judgment

"And at that time your people shall be delivered, Every one who is found written in the book. And many of those who sleep in the dust of the earth shall awake, Some to everlasting life, Some to shame and everlasting contempt."
(Daniel 12:1–2)

=

And I saw the dead, small and great, standing before God, and books were opened. And another book was opened, which is the Book of Life. And the dead were judged according to their works, by the things which were written in the books. The sea gave up the dead who were in it, and Death and Hades delivered up the dead who were in them. And they were judged, each one according to his works.
(Revelation 20:12–13)

Prophecies of the opening of the Book of Life and the resurrection of the dead

"Lift up your eyes to the heavens, and look on the earth beneath. For the heavens will vanish away like smoke, the earth will grow old like a garment, and those who dwell in it will die in like manner; but My salvation will be forever, and My righteousness will not be abolished. . . . For behold, I create new heavens and a new earth; and the former shall not be remembered or come to mind."
(Isaiah 51:6, 65:17)

=

Now I saw a new heaven and a new earth, for the first heaven and the first earth had passed away. Also there was no more sea.
(Revelation 21:1)

Prophecies of the passing away of the first heaven and the first earth and the arrival of a new heaven and a new earth

We previously determined that the remaining Old Testament prophecies had been fulfilled in the first century. Therefore, in the chart above, the prophecies from the books of Daniel and Isaiah have been fulfilled. There's no indication in the Bible that those were *pictures* of the events; those were prophecies of the *actual* events. Those *actual* Second Coming prophecies—like the rest of the remaining Old Testament prophecies—were fulfilled in the first century.

From the chart above, if we were to say that those parallel prophecies from Revelation are still unfulfilled, that would mean that, one day, the Second Coming will occur again, the day of judgment will occur again, the opening of the Book of Life will occur again, the resurrection of all the dead will occur again, heaven and earth will pass away again, and an even newer heaven and earth will arrive. It would be illogical, of course, to believe that the very same Second Coming events were going to occur again. The fulfillment of those actual events occurred in the first century—in "the days of vengeance"—and there's no indication in the Bible that those same events will occur again someday.

Therefore, from the previous chart:

- when Daniel 7:13–14, 18 was fulfilled in the first century, Revelation 14:14–16, 19 (its parallel) was also fulfilled, because Daniel and Revelation are referring to the same event—the Second Coming and the day of judgment;

- when Daniel 12:1–2 was fulfilled in the first century, Revelation 20:12–13 (its parallel) was also fulfilled, because Daniel and Revelation are referring to the same event—the opening of the Book of Life and the resurrection of the dead; and

- when Isaiah 51:6, 65:17 was fulfilled in the first century, Revelation 21:1 (its parallel) was also fulfilled, because Isaiah and Revelation are referring to the same event— the passing away of the first heaven and the first earth and the arrival of a new heaven and a new earth.

The actual events of the Second Coming occurred in the first century, so if we were to say that the prophecies in Revelation have not yet been fulfilled, we'd be making some illogical statements, such as the following:

"The prophecies of the Second Coming and the day of judgment have been fulfilled, but those prophecies *haven't* been fulfilled." (That would be saying that those events have occurred, but they also *haven't* occurred—which would be an illogical statement.)

"The prophecies of the opening of the Book of Life and the resurrection of the dead have been fulfilled, but those prophecies *haven't* been fulfilled." (That would be saying that those events have occurred, but they also *haven't* occurred— which would be an illogical statement.)

"The prophecies of the passing away of the first heaven and the first earth and the arrival of a new heaven and a new earth have been fulfilled, but those prophecies *haven't* been fulfilled." (That would be saying that those events have occurred, but they also *haven't* occurred—which would be an illogical statement.)

All of the prophecies in Revelation were fulfilled in the first century—the same time that all of the remaining Old Testament prophecies were fulfilled. All prophecy has been fulfilled; there are no future prophecies yet to be fulfilled.

In Revelation 21:1 in our preceding chart, John wrote that he "saw a new heaven and a new earth, for the first heaven and the first earth had passed away." This is significant for two reasons:

1. The passing away of heaven and earth meant that all prophecy had been fulfilled. We know this because of Jesus' statement in Matthew 5:18 from His Sermon on the Mount: "For assuredly, I say to you, till heaven and earth pass away, one jot or one tittle will by no means pass from the law till all is fulfilled." That would mean that all prophecy would have to be fulfilled before heaven and earth would pass away; therefore, whenever heaven and earth *did* pass away, all prophecy would have been fulfilled.

2. The passing away of heaven and earth is also significant because we had determined that heaven and earth passed away in the first century. As we learned in the previous paragraph, all prophecy would have to be fulfilled before heaven and earth would pass away; therefore, when heaven and earth *did* pass away in the first century, all prophecy would have been fulfilled. Since all prophecy was fulfilled in the first century, there are no future prophecies yet to be fulfilled. Every prophecy in the Bible has been fulfilled.

The passing away of heaven and earth is figurative, covenantal language describing the end of the age—the end of the Mosaic age and the end of Judaism. It was God's destruction of the temple, the Levitical priesthood, and the sacrificial system by means of the first-century tribulation by the Roman armies.

In the Olivet Discourse, in Matthew 24:35, Jesus said, "Heaven and earth will pass away, but My words will by no means pass away." Jesus was stating that the law of Moses—"heaven and earth"/the old covenant—would pass away (in the days of first-century tribulation), but the law of Christ—"My words"/the new covenant—would never pass away.

We can also see the equivalence between "heaven and earth" and the law of Moses in Matthew 5:17–18, where Jesus said, "Do not think that I came to destroy the Law or the Prophets [the law of Moses]. I did not come to destroy but to fulfill. For assuredly, I say to you, till heaven and earth [the law of Moses] pass away, one jot or one tittle will by no means pass from the law till all is fulfilled." Based on Jesus' statements, every aspect of the law of Moses would exist until heaven and earth passed away. If one believes that "heaven and earth" is referring to the literal heaven and earth, and since they haven't literally passed away, that would mean that Judaism still exists—including the physical temple, the Levitical priesthood, and the animal sacrifices. However, since Judaism no longer exists, that means that "heaven and earth"—as a Jewish idiom—*has* passed away.

We'll examine this covenantal language in more detail later in this book.

An interesting study would be to try to determine the point at which heaven and earth passed away. Here are some possibilities:

- In Matthew 5:18 (as we saw above), Jesus said, "For assuredly, I say to you, till heaven and earth pass away, one jot or one tittle will by no means pass from the law till all is fulfilled." From our discussion above, that would indicate that all prophecy would have to be fulfilled before the first heaven and the first earth would pass away; therefore, whenever heaven and earth *did* pass away, all prophecy would have been fulfilled. That would indicate that the sequence was 1) all remaining prophecy would be fulfilled, then 2) heaven and earth would pass away.

- 2 Peter 3:7 says, "But the heavens and the earth which are now preserved by the same word, are reserved for fire until the day of judgment and perdition of ungodly men." That would seem to indicate that heaven and earth would pass away *at* the day of judgment, not before or after; heaven and earth would pass away at the same time that all remaining prophecy would be fulfilled.

- Revelation 20:11 says, "Then I saw a great white throne and Him who sat on it, from whose face the earth and the heaven fled away." That verse would appear to be the passing away of heaven and earth. The rest of the chapter is about the opening of the Book of Life and the resurrection of the dead and their final judgment. That sequence would seem to be the reverse of the above bulleted section; in Revelation, that sequence would seem to be that 1) heaven and earth would pass away, then 2) all remaining prophecy would be fulfilled.

- After the end of Revelation 20 (in the bulleted section above), the next verse (Revelation 21:1) says, "Now I saw a new heaven and a new earth, for the first heaven and the first earth had passed away. Also there was no more sea." It's possible that this verse, not Revelation 20:11 (above), is where the first heaven and the first earth would pass away. If that's correct, Revelation 20:11 could mean that heaven and earth was in the *process* of passing away, and it didn't pass away until Revelation 21:1. That would seem to indicate the same sequence as the first bulleted section: 1) all remaining prophecy would be fulfilled, then 2) heaven and earth would pass away.

Even if we can't determine exactly when heaven and earth passed away, we can see that the timing of heaven and earth passing away is closely connected to the timing of the day of judgment (and therefore, the Second Coming). We can make the following logical sequence:

1. The passing away of heaven and earth is closely connected to the day of judgment and the Second Coming.

2. The passing away of heaven and earth is equivalent to the destruction of Judaism.

3. Therefore, the destruction of Judaism is closely connected to the day of judgment and the Second Coming.

4. The destruction of Judaism occurred in the first century.

5. Since the destruction of Judaism occurred in the first century, and since the destruction of Judaism is closely connected to the day of judgment and the Second Coming, that means that the day of judgment and the Second Coming occurred in the first century.

* * * * *

Another way we know that all prophecy was fulfilled in the first century is because of the first-century fulfillment of Jesus' prophecy in Matthew 24:14 from His Olivet Discourse: "And this gospel of the kingdom will be preached in all the world as a witness to all the nations, and then the end will come *[the Mosaic age would end (the first heaven and the first earth would pass away) and thus all prophecy would have been fulfilled]*." The gospel was indeed preached "in all the world" in the first century, as Paul wrote in some of his letters: "the prophetic Scriptures *[that were]* made known to all nations" (Romans 16:26); "'Their sound *[the preaching of the gospel]* has gone out to all the earth, and their words to the ends of the world'" (Romans 10:18, fulfilling the prophecy from Psalm 19:4); "*[the gospel]* has come to you, as it has also in all the world" (Colossians 1:6). Titus confirmed Paul's words: "the grace of God that brings salvation has appeared to all men" (Titus 2:11). Since the gospel had been preached "in all the world" in the first century, the end would then come soon in that first century, as Peter confirmed in 1 Peter 4:5 and 7: "*[Jesus]* is ready to judge the living and the dead . . . the end of all things is at hand."

The fact that all prophecy has been fulfilled is significant. Since most of the New Testament books contain prophecy, and since all remaining prophecy was fulfilled around A.D. 70, that means that any New Testament book containing prophecy was written before A.D. 70—including Revelation.

Revelation 17:10 identifies when the book of Revelation was written: "'There are also seven kings. Five have fallen, one is, and the other has not yet come. And when he comes, he must continue a short time.'" When we interpret the kings as the Caesars of Rome, the five that had fallen were Julius, Augustus, Tiberius, Caligula, and Claudius; the "one is" (the one who was currently reigning at the time Revelation was written) was Nero; and the other who had not yet come to power for his short reign would be Galba.

Most of Revelation is basically John's version of the Olivet Discourse, containing more detail than the version in Matthew, Mark, and Luke. Most of Revelation uses figurative, symbolic language, and like the Olivet Discourse, it's not chronological and includes events that were to occur up until around A.D. 70. That would necessitate Revelation being written before A.D. 70, and since Nero reigned from A.D. 54–68, that pre-A.D. 70 date for its writing fits perfectly. Most Christians believe that Revelation was written near the end of the reign of Roman Emperor Domitian, around the year A.D. 95. However, since Revelation's internal evidence shows that its prophecies were to be fulfilled no later than around A.D. 70, that A.D. 95 dating for Revelation would have to be rejected. Whenever there's a contradiction between an external source and the Bible's internal evidence, the latter should be favored.

We can determine that Revelation's prophecies were to be fulfilled in the first century by identifying those same prophecies in other parts of the Bible, and then, if it's clear that those same prophecies were to be fulfilled in the first century, that means that Revelation's parallel prophecies would also be fulfilled in the first century. For example, by comparing Luke 21:22–23 (followed by verse 32), Luke 23:28–30, and Revelation 6:15–17, we can determine that the Revelation passage was to be fulfilled in the first century:

"For these are the days of vengeance, that all things which are written may be fulfilled. But woe to those who are pregnant and to those who are nursing babies in those days! For there will be great distress in the land and wrath upon this people.... Assuredly, I say to you, this generation will by no means pass away till all things take place." *(Luke 21:22–23 and 32)*	But Jesus, turning to them, said, "Daughters of Jerusalem, do not weep for Me, but weep for yourselves and for your children. For indeed the days are coming in which they will say, 'Blessed are the barren, wombs that never bore, and breasts which never nursed!' Then they will begin 'to say to the mountains, "Fall on us!" and to the hills, "Cover us!"'" *(Luke 23:28–30)*	And the kings of the earth, the great men, the rich men, the commanders, the mighty men, every slave and every free man, hid themselves in the caves and in the rocks of the mountains, and said to the mountains and rocks, "Fall on us and hide us from the face of Him who sits on the throne and from the wrath of the Lamb! For the great day of His wrath has come, and who is able to stand?" *(Revelation 6:15–17)*

In the Luke 21 passage in the chart, Jesus said, "But woe to those who are pregnant and to those who are nursing babies in those days!" That event occurred in the first century because it occurred "in those days"—in the first-century "days of vengeance" and within "this *[first-century]* generation" (all of those time statements are in that Luke 21 passage).

In the Luke 23 passage in the chart, we can determine that Jesus was referring to first-century events because the "daughters of Jerusalem" were to weep for their children—who would be living in that first century. Also, since the "woe to those who are pregnant" verse from Luke 21 was a first-century event, the comparable verse in Luke 23 would also be a first-century event: "Blessed are the barren, wombs that never bore, and breasts which never nursed!" Therefore, the next verse in Luke 23 would also be a first-century event: "Then they will begin 'to say to the mountains, "Fall on us!" and to the hills, "Cover us!"'"

In Revelation 6 in the chart, the people in that passage said, "Fall on us and hide us from the face of Him who sits on the throne and from the wrath of the Lamb!" This is comparable to the "Fall on us!" phrase from Luke 23 in the chart. Since that Luke 23 event occurred in the first century, that comparable Revelation event also occurred in the first century. Also, "the great day of His wrath has come" in the Revelation passage is referring to the first-century great tribulation because it's the same first-century "days of vengeance" as in the Luke 21 passage in the chart. Therefore, Revelation 6:15–17 in the chart is referring to events that occurred in the first century.

When we understand that the prophecies in Revelation were fulfilled in the first century, we can identify its first-century events and people. Kurt M. Simmons' book, *The Consummation of the Ages*, was the basis for the commentary on the following Revelation passages:

- *"Then I saw an angel coming down from heaven, having the key to the bottomless pit and a great chain in his hand. He laid hold of the dragon, that serpent of old, who is the Devil and Satan, and bound him for a thousand years; and he cast him into the bottomless pit, and shut him up, and set a seal on him, so that he should deceive the nations no more till the thousand years were finished. But after these things he must be released for a little while."* (Revelation 20:1–3)

  This verse symbolizes the relative peace that Christians had under the reign of Roman Emperor Claudius, who enforced a law stating that Christianity was a legitimate religion so that Christians would be free from punishment. Claudius had the figurative key to bind the dragon/Devil/Satan (referring to imperial Rome) for a symbolic thousand years, thus preventing persecution of the church, especially by Roman officials.

The "thousand years" is used here as a comparative and round number:

- It's comparative in that the twenty-six literal years that the dragon was bound was a long time (from about A.D. 33, when Paul was converted to Christianity, until about A.D. 64, when Nero began to persecute the church) compared to the smaller time of 3½ years that it was loosed (the period of time that Nero persecuted the church).

- The "thousand years" is round in that it represents completeness—the dragon was bound for a time, and when that time was complete, it was loosed.

(*Consummation*, pp. 362–68)

- "*Now when the thousand years have expired, Satan will be released from his prison and will go out to deceive the nations which are in the four corners of the earth, Gog and Magog, to gather them together to battle, whose number is as the sand of the sea.*" (Revelation 20:7–8)

The loosing of the dragon/Devil/Satan/imperial Rome refers to Nero's persecution of the church. When loosed from the bottomless pit, Rome gathers the nations together for battle. These nations are referred to "Gog and Magog" and are equivalent to the peoples and nations included within the ten provinces of Rome and the beast. This battle refers to the forces of the Romans and Jews allied against the church.

The battle of Gog and Magog is the same as the battle of Armageddon (Revelation 16:13–16). It's important to make this connection because this demonstrates how the book of Revelation is not in chronological order. Revelation will sometimes begin a theme, and then later, in another chapter, that theme will reappear and will continue to progress until it reaches a conclusion. It's a mistake to see the book of Revelation in terms of chronological order rather than a progression of themes. The themes progress toward a climax, but not in chronological order. In Revelation, there's a definite progression toward a climax, but it reaches the climax only after retracing its steps several times, providing a fuller understanding of the events leading to the end. There's both progression and retrogression: progression because with each series of judgments there are also introduced new characters and circumstances bound up in the events marking the end, and retrogression because the seals, trumpets, vials, etc., overlap somewhat.

(*Consummation*, pp. 378–85)

- "*And he* [the beast/Nero] *was given a mouth speaking great things and blasphemies, and he was given authority to continue for forty-two months.*" (Revelation 13:5)

Nero was given authority to attack the church for forty-two months or 3½ years; his persecution of the church began in 11/64 and continued until 6/68 when he committed suicide. The joining of Nero and Jewish leaders into a partnership to destroy Christians fits the picture found in Revelation 17:3–7 where there's an alliance between the beast and the harlot (Jerusalem).

(*Consummation*, p. 258)

- *"'And they will tread the holy city underfoot for forty-two months.'"* (Revelation 11:2b)

Jesus spoke of this in His Olivet Discourse when He said in Luke 21:24b, "And Jerusalem will be trampled by Gentiles until the times of the Gentiles are fulfilled." The "times" that God granted the Gentiles (the Romans) is stated in the Revelation verse as forty-two months—the last 3½ years of Jerusalem's existence (A.D. 2/67 to 8/70) before being completely leveled by Rome ("trampled by Gentiles" from that verse in Luke). This also perfectly fits Daniel 12:7, which, as we'll see in the next chapter of this book, shows that Daniel 12 was prophesying about first-century events:

> Then I heard the man clothed in linen, who was above the waters of the river, when he held up his right hand and his left hand to heaven, and swore by Him who lives forever, that it shall be for a time, times, and half a time; and when the power of the holy people has been completely shattered, all these things shall be finished.

The forty-two-month period in that Revelation 11:2b verse is the same period as the 1,260 days that the two witnesses prophesied, clothed in sackcloth (Revelation 11:3). However, that forty-two-month period is not the same as the forty-two-month period in Revelation 13:5 (that we discussed in the previous bulleted section); that 3½ years in Revelation 13:5 was the length of Nero's persecution of the church from 11/64 to 6/68, while the 3½ years in Revelation 11:2b (in this bulleted section) was the length of Rome's destruction of Jerusalem from 2/67 to 8/70.

(Consummation, pp. 213–15)

- *"'The merchants of these things, who became rich by her, will stand at a distance for fear of her torment, weeping and wailing, and saying, "'"Alas, alas, that great city that was clothed in fine linen, purple, and scarlet, and adorned with gold and precious stones and pearls! For in one hour such great riches came to nothing."'" "'Every shipmaster, all who travel by ship, sailors, and as many as trade on the sea, stood at a distance and cried out when they saw the smoke of her burning, saying, "'"What is like this great city?"'*

  "'They threw dust on their heads and cried out, weeping and wailing, and saying, "'"Alas, alas, that great city, in which all who had ships on the sea became rich by her wealth! For in one hour she is made desolate."'

  "'Rejoice over her, O heaven, and you holy apostles and prophets, for God has avenged you on her!'" (Revelation 18:15–20)

The description of the attire of the harlot (Jerusalem) is equivalent to the trimming, veil, and stones of the temple that adorned Jerusalem, drawing so many to her from around the world. Herod's temple, which had just been completed in A.D. 63, was razed to the ground.

The mourners in this passage were those who shipped and transported goods to Jerusalem's markets. They were not mourning for Jerusalem's suffering; they were mourning for their loss of revenue. The harlot—Jerusalem—had been made desolate.

(*Consummation*, pp. 342–44)

- "'And in her was found the blood of prophets and saints, and of all who were slain on the earth.'" (Revelation 18:24)

This language corresponds exactly with Jesus' statement regarding Jerusalem in the parallel verses below from Matthew 23 and Luke 11 (with emphasis added):

"'Therefore, indeed, I send you prophets, wise men, and scribes: some of them you will kill and crucify, and some of them you will scourge in your synagogues and persecute from city to city, that on you may come all the righteous blood shed on the earth, from the blood of righteous Abel to the blood of Zechariah, son of Berechiah, whom you murdered between the temple and the altar. Assuredly, I say to you, all these things will come upon **this generation**.'" *(Matthew 23:34–36)*	=	"Therefore the wisdom of God also said, 'I will send them prophets and apostles, and some of them they will kill and persecute,' that the blood of all the prophets which was shed from the foundation of the world may be required of **this generation**, from the blood of Abel to the blood of Zechariah who perished between the altar and the temple. Yes, I say to you, it shall be required of **this generation**." *(Luke 11:49–51)*

In those passages from Matthew and Luke, Jesus prophesied that "this generation" (the first-century generation of the Jews) would be held accountable for all that shed blood. It would be God's "days of vengeance" (Luke 21:22). That vengeance would occur in the destruction of Jerusalem; therefore, in the Revelation verse above, that same shed blood—"the blood of prophets and saints, and of all who were slain on the earth"—verifies that the Revelation verse is referring to that first-century "days of vengeance."

(*Consummation*, p. 346)

- *"And he said to me, 'Do not seal the words of the prophecy of this book, for the time is at hand.'"* (Revelation 22:10)

When Daniel had received the visions, he was told to "'shut up the words, and seal the book until the time of the end.'" In the Revelation verse above, the time was now "at hand"; the end of all prophecy was near, so John was told "not *[to]* seal the words of the prophecy of this book."

(*Consummation*, pp. 422–24)

This leads into the next verse from Revelation:

- "'*He who is unjust, let him be unjust still; he who is filthy, let him be filthy still; he who is righteous, let him be righteous still; he who is holy, let him be holy still.*'" (Revelation 22:11)

The day of Christ's return was so near that there was almost no time left for people to change: the judge was at the door (James 5:7–9) ready to judge (1 Peter 4:5). In fact, Hebrews 10:37 said that in a very, very little while (*mikron hoson hoson* in the original Greek), He who was coming would come. This verse from Revelation indicates that the door was about to be shut against Israel, pictured in Jesus' parable in Matthew 25 where the door of the wedding was shut to the five foolish virgins who had gone to buy oil for their lamps.

(*Consummation*, p. 424)

In the Olivet Discourse accounts from Matthew, Mark, and Luke, the Second Coming prophecy would be fulfilled in about forty years, but at the time Revelation was written, the Second Coming was one of the "things which must shortly take place . . . for the time is near" (Revelation 1:1 and 1:3). That first chapter of Revelation announced the nearness, and the last chapter was a bookend that *emphasized* that nearness: "the things which must shortly take place" and "'the time is at hand'"(Revelation 22:6 and 22:10). The events that were to occur shortly concerned the destruction of Judaism and its capital (Jerusalem), as well as the coming of the fully established kingdom in which the faithful would receive redemption.

Jesus said in Revelation 22:20, "Surely I am coming quickly." Most Christians believe that this means Jesus would return with quickness and suddenness. However, Thayer includes a parenthetical "without delay" in his definition: "quickly, speedily, (without delay)." When something occurs without delay, it means that it can occur soon in time, promptly, or shortly. At the time Revelation was written, the Second Coming would be one of the "things which must shortly take place"; therefore, Jesus would be "coming quickly"—soon and without delay.

* * * * *

Most Christians still might say that Jesus could not have been prophesying that the *actual* Second Coming would occur in the first century because even *He* didn't know when the Second Coming would occur, as He said in the Olivet Discourse in Mark 13:32: "But of that day and hour no one knows, not even the angels in heaven, nor the Son, but only the Father."

It's a Scriptural truth that the *exact* day and hour would not be known, but the *approximate* time would be known because, in the Olivet Discourse, Jesus prophesied about the events that would lead up to the Second Coming: wars and rumors of wars, famines, pestilences, earthquakes, false christs and false prophets, the abomination of desolation, and the great tribulation. Then, after that great tribulation of the first century, the *actual* Second Coming (and not a *picture* of it) would occur.

By telling His disciples about the events that would lead up to the Second Coming, Jesus was answering all of their questions from Matthew 24:3: "Tell us, when will these things be [the destruction of the temple]? And what will be the sign of Your coming, and of the end of the age?" The following will show that Jesus had answered each question.

- *Tell us, when will these things be* [the destruction of the temple]?

  Jesus told them the events that would lead up to the destruction of the temple: wars and rumors of wars, famines, pestilences, earthquakes, false christs and false prophets, the abomination of desolation, and then the great tribulation, which would include the destruction of the temple.

- *And what will be the sign of Your coming*

  As we mentioned before, Jesus told them the events that would lead up to the Second Coming: wars and rumors of wars, famines, pestilences, earthquakes, false christs and false prophets, the abomination of desolation, the great tribulation, and then, after that great tribulation of the first century, the *actual* Second Coming (and not a *picture* of it) would occur.

- *and* [what will be the sign] *of the end of the age*

  In Matthew 13, Jesus told the parable about a man who planted good seed in his field, and while he and his men were asleep, his enemy planted tares (weeds) among his wheat. In verses 39–41 of that parable, He said,

  ³⁹The enemy who sowed them *[the tares]* is the devil, the harvest is the end of the age, and the reapers are the angels. ⁴⁰Therefore as the tares are gathered and burned in the fire, so it will be at

the end of this age. ⁴¹The Son of Man will send out His angels, and they will gather out of His kingdom all things that offend, and those who practice lawlessness,"

That parable taught that the spiritual harvest would occur at the end of the age. In the Olivet Discourse, Jesus prophesied that after the great tribulation of the first century, the harvest would occur: "He will send His angels with a great sound of a trumpet, and they will gather together His elect from the four winds, from one end of heaven to the other." Since the harvest would occur at the end of the age, and since the harvest occurred in the first century, that means that the end of the age occurred in the first century. The harvest was one of the events of the Second Coming, so by answering the question "And what will be the sign of Your coming," He had also answered the question "and [what will be the sign] of the end of the age." The "end of the age" was the end of the Mosaic age, the end of the Mosaic covenant, and the end of Judaism—not the end of planet Earth. We'll discuss the phrase "end of the age" later in this book.

Most Christians believe that the first part of Matthew 24:3 ("Tell us, when will these things be?") is referring to the destruction of the temple, but they believe that the second part ("And what will be the sign of Your coming, and of the end of the age?") is about a literal, bodily return of Jesus that has not yet occurred. This book demonstrated, however, that all three events occurred in the first century: the destruction of the temple, the Second Coming, and the end of the age.

Let's create a chart that summarizes our study of Luke 21:22 and 32, Matthew 24:30–31, and Mark 13:26–27:

> "For these are the days of vengeance, that all things which are written may be fulfilled. . . . Assuredly, I say to you, this generation will by no means pass away till all things take place."
> *(Luke 21:22 and 32)*

All remaining prophecies from the Scriptures would be fulfilled in the first century.

> "and they will see the Son of Man coming on the clouds of heaven with power and great glory. And He will send His angels with a great sound of a trumpet, and they will gather together His elect from the four winds, from one end of heaven to the other."
> *(Matthew 24:30–31)*

=

> "Then they will see the Son of Man coming in the clouds with great power and glory. And then He will send His angels, and gather together His elect from the four winds, from the farthest part of earth to the farthest part of heaven."
> *(Mark 13:26–27)*

In the Olivet Discourse, Jesus made this prophecy about the Second Coming. The Second Coming was one of the prophecies from the Scriptures. All remaining prophecies from the Scriptures would be fulfilled in the first century, so that means that the Second Coming—like the rest of the remaining prophecies—was fulfilled in the first century.

On the next page, let's add to our ongoing chart the Olivet Discourse verses that appeared at the beginning of this chapter. Let's continue to keep the chart on one page by presenting just the key points from the previous version of that ongoing chart.

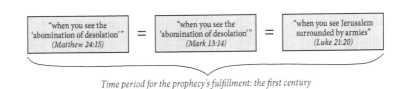

| "when you see the 'abomination of desolation'" (Matthew 24:15) | = | "when you see the 'abomination of desolation'" (Mark 13:14) | = | "when you see Jerusalem surrounded by armies" (Luke 21:20) |

Time period for the prophecy's fulfillment: the first century

| "then let those who are in Judea flee to the mountains" (Matthew 24:16) | = | "then let those who are in Judea flee to the mountains" (Mark 13:14) | = | "Then let those who are in Judea flee to the mountains" (Luke 21:21) |

Time period for the fulfillment: still the first century

| "For then there will be great tribulation" (Matthew 24:21) | = | "For in those days there will be tribulation" (Mark 13:19) | = | "there will be great distress" (Luke 21:23) |

Time period for the fulfillment: still the first century

| "Immediately after the tribulation of those days the sun will be darkened, and the moon will not give its light; the stars will fall from heaven, and the powers of the heavens will be shaken. Then the sign of the Son of Man will appear in heaven, and then all the tribes of the earth will mourn," (Matthew 24:29–30) | = | "But in those days, after that tribulation, the sun will be darkened, and the moon will not give its light; the stars of heaven will fall, and the powers in the heavens will be shaken." (Mark 13:24–25) |

Time period for the fulfillment: still the first century

| "and they will see the Son of Man coming on the clouds of heaven with power and great glory. And He will send His angels with a great sound of a trumpet, and they will gather together His elect from the four winds, from one end of heaven to the other." (Matthew 24:30–31) | = | "Then they will see the Son of Man coming in the clouds with great power and glory. And then He will send His angels, and gather together His elect from the four winds, from the farthest part of earth to the farthest part of heaven." (Mark 13:26–27) |

Time period for the fulfillment: still the first century

The Second Coming occurred in the first century because that's when the events of the Second Coming occurred: Jesus coming on the clouds, Jesus sending His angels, the trumpet, and the gathering (spiritual harvest/judgment) of God's faithful people.

By using a logical, step-by-step approach, this book demonstrated that the Second Coming, the day of judgment, and the end of all prophecy have already occurred—in the first century. The Second Coming occurred in the first century because that's when the events of the Second Coming occurred: Jesus coming on the clouds, Jesus sending His angels, the trumpet, and the gathering (the spiritual harvest/judgment) of God's faithful people.

Since there's no record that Jesus physically came on or in literal clouds in the first century, no trumpet sounded, and none of the faithful were physically gathered by the angels, none of those events were literal. Jesus was using idiomatic language—figures of speech that are common to a particular society, but will be misunderstood by a different society when taken literally.

The Second Coming will be misunderstood if those events are interpreted literally. The Second Coming is not a future event where Jesus will physically return on the clouds, a literal trumpet will sound, the faithful will physically rise to meet Jesus in the air, and the dead will physically rise from their graves; instead, that symbolic, idiomatic language describes the first-century fulfillment of God's plan: the restoration of fellowship between God and man through God's granting of redemption. We'll later examine some of the Second Coming events to see how they are actually figurative and symbolic, and not literal.

In the next chapter, we'll examine Daniel 12 to show that it supports that first-century timing of the Second Coming and the day of judgment.

Daniel 12

Let's examine the entire chapter of Daniel 12 to show that it—like the Olivet Discourse—supports that first-century timing of the Second Coming and the day of judgment.

> ¹"At that time Michael shall stand up,
> The great prince who stands watch over the sons of your people;
> And there shall be a time of trouble,
> Such as never was since there was a nation,
> Even to that time.
> And at that time your people shall be delivered,
> Every one who is found written in the book.
> ²And many of those who sleep in the dust of the earth shall awake,
> Some to everlasting life,
> Some to shame and everlasting contempt.
> ³Those who are wise shall shine
> Like the brightness of the firmament,
> And those who turn many to righteousness
> Like the stars forever and ever.

> ⁴"But you, Daniel, shut up the words, and seal the book until the time of the end; many shall run to and fro, and knowledge shall increase."

> ⁵Then I, Daniel, looked; and there stood two others, one on this riverbank and the other on that riverbank. ⁶And one said to the man clothed in linen, who was above the waters of the river, "How long shall the fulfillment of these wonders be?"

⁷Then I heard the man clothed in linen, who was above the waters of the river, when he held up his right hand and his left hand to heaven, and swore by Him who lives forever, that it shall be for a time, times, and half a time; and when the power of the holy people has been completely shattered, all these things shall be finished.

⁸Although I heard, I did not understand. Then I said, "My lord, what shall be the end of these things?"

⁹And he said, "Go your way, Daniel, for the words are closed up and sealed till the time of the end. ¹⁰Many shall be purified, made white, and refined, but the wicked shall do wickedly; and none of the wicked shall understand, but the wise shall understand.

¹¹"And from the time that the daily sacrifice is taken away, and the abomination of desolation is set up, there shall be one thousand two hundred and ninety days. ¹²Blessed is he who waits, and comes to the one thousand three hundred and thirty-five days.

¹³"But you, go your way till the end; for you shall rest, and will arise to your inheritance at the end of the days."

The chapter begins with "At that time," which means that there's a connection between the time period of Daniel 12 and the last part of Daniel 11. There are various opinions regarding the identity of the person in those Daniel 11 passages, including Antiochus IV Epiphanes, Julius Caesar, and Herod the Great. Instead of studying Daniel 11 to try to identify that person, let's focus on Daniel 12, where we see parallels to the Olivet Discourse. Let's start by comparing the first two lines of Daniel 12 to Matthew 24:16–18 and Mark 13:14b–16:

"At that time Michael shall stand up, The great prince who stands watch over the sons of your people;" *(Daniel 12:1)*	"then let those who are in Judea flee to the mountains. Let him who is on the housetop not go down to take anything out of his house. And let him who is in the field not go back to get his clothes." *(Matthew 24:16–18)*	"then let those who are in Judea flee to the mountains. Let him who is on the housetop not go down into the house, nor enter to take anything out of his house. And let him who is in the field not go back to get his clothes." *(Mark 13:14b–16)*

Time period for the prophecy's fulfillment: the first century

Those three passages are connected because they are a prophecy about how the Christians would be protected at the time of the great tribulation of the Jews. According to traditional history, no Christian perished in the destruction of Jerusalem.

The next parallel we see between Daniel 12 and the Olivet Discourse is the prophecy of the great tribulation of the first century:

"And there shall be a time of trouble, Such as never was since there was a nation, Even to that time." *(Daniel 12:1)*	=	"For then there will be great tribulation, such as has not been since the beginning of the world until this time, no, nor ever shall be." *(Matthew 24:21)*	=	"For in those days there will be tribulation, such as has not been since the beginning of the creation which God created until this time, nor ever shall be." *(Mark 13:19)*	=	"For there will be great distress in the land and wrath upon this people." *(Luke 21:23)*

Time period for the prophecy's fulfillment: the first century

The next prophecy we see in Daniel 12 is about the events that would occur "at that time" (at the time of the first-century tribulation). It would be the time of the final judgment and the resurrection of the dead—events of the Second Coming. As we saw earlier in this book, those verses from Daniel are a parallel to Revelation 20:12-13:

"And at that time your people shall be delivered, Every one who is found written in the book. And many of those who sleep in the dust of the earth shall awake, Some to everlasting life, Some to shame and everlasting contempt." (Daniel 12:1-2)	=	And I saw the dead, small and great, standing before God, and books were opened. And another book was opened, which is the Book of Life. And the dead were judged according to their works, by the things which were written in the books. The sea gave up the dead who were in it, and Death and Hades delivered up the dead who were in them. And they were judged, each one according to his works. (Revelation 20:12-13)

The phrase "many of those who sleep" in the above passage from Daniel might seem that it's not referring to the general resurrection of *all* the dead; it might seem to be indicating that only *many* were resurrected. However, it actually *is* referring to the resurrection of *all* the dead because the "many" from Daniel 12 were given *final* judgment (*everlasting* life or *everlasting* contempt), and the final judgment was given to the general resurrection of *all* the dead at the Second Coming.

The meaning of "many"—all—in that verse is equivalent to the meaning of "many" in Romans 5:15 ("for if by the one man's [Adam's] offense many died") and Romans 5:19 ("for as by one man's [Adam's] disobedience many were made sinners").

Our study of the Olivet Discourse showed that after the great tribulation of the first century, the events of the Second Coming occurred: Jesus sent His angels and they gathered together His elect (the spiritual harvest). That's a parallel to Daniel 12 because it, too, shows that after the tribulation, the events of the Second Coming would occur: the Book of Life would be opened and the dead would be resurrected spiritually—not bodily—for their final judgment. Therefore, Daniel 12 and the Olivet Discourse are in perfect agreement that the Second Coming would occur in the first century after the great tribulation. The following chart shows this connection between Daniel 12 and the Olivet Discourse.

"And there shall be a time of trouble, Such as never was since there was a nation, Even to that time." *(Daniel 12:1)*	=	"For then there will be great tribulation, such as has not been since the beginning of the world until this time, no, nor ever shall be." *(Matthew 24:21)*	=	"For in those days there will be tribulation, such as has not been since the beginning of the creation which God created until this time, nor ever shall be." *(Mark 13:19)*

Time period for the prophecy's fulfillment: the first century

"at that time" *(Daniel 12:1)*	"after the tribulation of those days" *(Matthew 24:29)*	"But in those days, after that tribulation" *(Mark 13:24)*

Time period for the fulfillment: still the first century

"your people shall be delivered, Every one who is found written in the book. And many of those who sleep in the dust of the earth shall awake, Some to everlasting life, Some to shame and everlasting contempt." *(Daniel 12:1–2)*	"they *[all the tribes of the earth]* will see the Son of Man coming on the clouds of heaven with power and great glory. And He will send His angels with a great sound of a trumpet, and they will gather together His elect from the four winds, from one end of heaven to the other." *(Matthew 24:30–31)*	"Then they will see the Son of Man coming in the clouds with great power and glory. And then He will send His angels, and gather together His elect from the four winds, from the farthest part of earth to the farthest part of heaven." *(Mark 13:26–27)*

Time period for the fulfillment: still the first century

Like the Olivet Discourse, Daniel 12 was prophesying about the *actual* Second Coming; there's no indication that Daniel 12 was prophesying about a *picture* of it. Daniel 12 prophesied that in the days of the "time of trouble" (the first-century tribulation of the Jews), "your people shall be delivered, every one who is found written in the book" and "many of those who sleep in the dust of the earth shall awake, some to everlasting life, some to shame and everlasting contempt." Those are *actual events* of the Second Coming—the opening of the Book of Life and the resurrection and judgment of the dead—so Daniel 12 was prophesying that the *actual events* of the Second Coming would occur in that first-century "time of trouble" (the great tribulation). The *actual* Second Coming occurred in the first century, but Jesus did not return visibly and bodily, and the dead did not physically rise from their graves; instead, like the Olivet Discourse prophecy about the coming of Jesus, Daniel 12 was using figurative language regarding the resurrection of the dead.

Since Daniel 12 prophesied that the events of the Second Coming would occur after the great tribulation, we can add another row to our table that has the following paraphrase in the second and third column heads: "In the first-century days of the great tribulation . . . all remaining prophecy from the Old Testament will be fulfilled—including the events of the Second Coming."

Verse	In the first-century days of the great tribulation . . .	all remaining prophecy from the Old Testament will be fulfilled—including the events of the Second Coming.
Luke 21:22	"For these are the days of vengeance,	that all things which are written may be fulfilled."
Matthew 24:21, 31	"For then there will be great tribulation . . .	And He will send His angels with a great sound of a trumpet, and they will gather together His elect from the four winds, from one end of heaven to the other."
Mark 13:19, 27	"For in those days there will be tribulation . . .	And then He will send His angels, and gather together His elect from the four winds, from the farthest part of earth to the farthest part of heaven."
Daniel 12:1–2	"And there shall be a time of trouble . . . And at that time . . .	your people shall be delivered, every one who is found written in the book. And many of those who sleep in the dust of the earth shall awake, some to everlasting life, some to shame and everlasting contempt."

In the verse from Luke in the table above, Jesus presented a general truth; in Daniel, we see an example that *demonstrated* that truth. In Luke, Jesus prophesied that all remaining prophecy from the Old Testament would be fulfilled in the days of the great tribulation; in Daniel, the prophecy about the resurrection and judgment of the dead—one of those remaining prophecies—would be fulfilled at that time. Since all remaining prophecy from the Old Testament would be fulfilled in the days of the first-century tribulation, and since the resurrection and judgment of the dead was one of those remaining prophecies, the *actual* resurrection of the dead—and not a *picture* of it—*had to occur* in the first century. If the resurrection and judgment of the dead *didn't* occur in the first century, then Jesus was mistaken when He said that "**all things** which are written may be fulfilled" in "the days of vengeance *[in the days of the first-century tribulation]*" *[emphasis added]*.

As we continue to read Daniel 12, we can see a connection between Daniel 12:2–3 and Matthew 13:39–43 (Jesus' explanation of the parable of the tares). Let's create a chart showing those passages:

"And many of those who sleep in the dust of the earth shall awake, some to everlasting life, some to shame and everlasting contempt. Those who are wise shall shine like the brightness of the firmament, and those who turn many to righteousness like the stars forever and ever." *(Daniel 12:2–3)*	"The enemy who sowed them *[the tares, or weeds]* is the devil, the harvest is the end of the age, and the reapers are the angels. Therefore as the tares are gathered and burned in the fire, so it will be at the end of this age. The Son of Man will send out His angels, and they will gather out of His kingdom all things that offend, and those who practice lawlessness, and will cast them into the furnace of fire. There will be wailing and gnashing of teeth. Then the righteous will shine forth as the sun in the kingdom of their Father. He who has ears to hear, let him hear!" *(Matthew 13:39–43)*

In Daniel 12 in the chart, Daniel was told, "Those who are wise shall shine like the brightness of the firmament, and those who turn many to righteousness like the stars forever and ever." This is a connection to Matthew 13 in the chart because Jesus referenced that prophecy when He said, "Then the righteous will shine forth as the sun in the kingdom of their Father."

We can identify an additional connection: in both Daniel 12 and Matthew 13 in the chart, the identical event—the Second Coming—precedes those "shine" prophecies:

- In Daniel, the resurrection and judgment of the dead would occur (an event of the Second Coming), and the "wise shall shine."

- In Matthew, Jesus would send out His angels for the final judgment (also an event of the Second Coming), and then the "righteous will shine."

In the chart, the connection between Daniel 12 and Matthew 13 is significant because of the time statements in Matthew 13: "the harvest is the end of the age" and "as the tares are gathered and burned in the fire, so it will be at the end of this age." As we studied earlier in this book, Jesus was living in the Mosaic age, so the harvest/the gathering and burning of the tares/Second Coming was to occur "at the end of *[the Mosaic]* age"—when Judaism was destroyed in the first century. Since those passages from Matthew 13 and Daniel 12 are parallel, and since the reaping/harvest—the Second Coming—in Matthew 13 was to occur in the first century, that means that the resurrection and judgment of the dead—the Second Coming—in Daniel 12 was to occur in the first century.

The next parallel we see between Daniel 12 and the Olivet Discourse is the connection between "it shall be for a time, times, and half a time" (Daniel 12:7) and "until the times of the Gentiles are fulfilled" (Luke 21:24b). Earlier in this book, we demonstrated that Daniel 12:7, Luke 21:24b, and Revelation 11:2b were parallel verses:

Then I heard the man clothed in linen, who was above the waters of the river, when he held up his right hand and his left hand to heaven, and swore by Him who lives forever, that it shall be for a time, times, and half a time; and when the power of the holy people has been completely shattered, all these things shall be finished. *(Daniel 12:7)*	=	"And Jerusalem will be trampled by Gentiles until the times of the Gentiles are fulfilled." *(Luke 21:24b)*	=	"And they will tread the holy city underfoot for forty-two months." *(Revelation 11:2b)*

In the verse from Luke in the chart above, the "times" that God granted the Gentiles (the Romans) is stated in the Revelation verse as forty-two months—the last 3½ years of Jerusalem's existence (A.D. 67–70) before being completely leveled by Rome ("trampled by Gentiles" from that verse in Luke).

In Daniel 12:7 in the chart, "the man clothed in linen" prophesied that "when the power of the holy people has been completely shattered, all these things shall be finished." Earlier, we saw that Daniel 12:1 was a prophecy about the first-century tribulation of the Jews, so, to stay within the context, "the power of the holy people" in Daniel 12:7 would be referring to the first-century Pharisees, scribes, and the other Judaizers, and their power would be "completely shattered" when the great tribulation had ended.

The shattering of the holy people's power from Daniel 12 is equivalent to the cosmic-destruction passages from the Olivet Discourse. From our study of the Olivet Discourse, we learned that apocalyptic language is used to dramatically describe the destruction of any given people's world—the downfall of a dynasty, the capture of a city, or the overthrow of a nation. The shattering of the holy people's power from Daniel 12 and the apocalyptic language from the Olivet Discourse are both describing the destruction of the first-century Jewish world—Judaism.

The next parallel we see between Daniel 12 and the Olivet Discourse is the event that would occur at the time of Jerusalem's destruction: the Second Coming. The prophecy in Daniel 12:7 said that "when the power of the holy people has been completely shattered, all these things shall be finished." The phrase "all these things" refers to the Second Coming events mentioned earlier in Daniel 12:1–2 of that chapter: the opening of the Book of Life and the resurrection of the dead for their final judgment. The following chart shows that connection between Daniel 12:7 and 12:1–2:

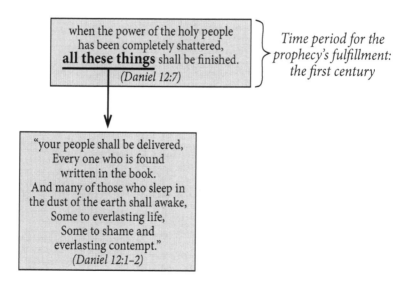

In the chart above, the phrase "all these things" from Daniel 12:7 refers back to Daniel 12:1-2 (indicated by the arrow in the chart), where we see prophecies of some of the Second Coming events: the opening of the Book of Life and the resurrection of the dead for their final judgment.

Therefore, "when the power of the holy people *[Judaism]* has been completely shattered, all these things *[the Second Coming]* shall be finished." The opening of the Book of Life and the resurrection of the dead—and therefore the Second Coming—would occur in the first century, after God had "completely shattered" Judaism.

Let's display that chart again, and let's compare it to a similar chart we had created during our study of the Olivet Discourse:

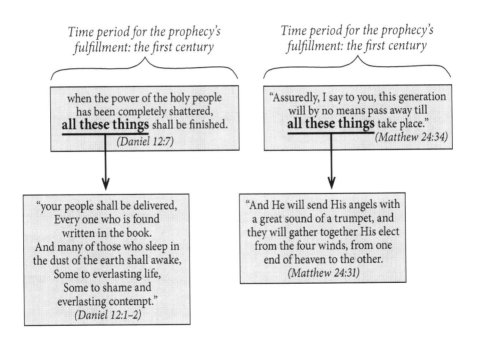

Some commentators believe that "generation" in Matthew 24:34 means "race." However, it can demonstrated that "generation" in that verse refers to the first-century "generation" of people:

The bottom row of the chart contains prophecies of the events of the Second Coming, so Daniel 12:1–2 and Matthew 24:31 would occur at about the same time. That allows us to create a logical sequence that shows the meaning of "generation" in Matthew 24:34. The sequence will start with Daniel 12:7 in the upper left of the chart, and the sequence will continue in a counter-clockwise path until we reach Matthew 24:34 in the upper right.

1. The "power of the holy people *[being]* completely shattered" is equivalent to the destruction of Judaism.

2. The destruction of Judaism occurred in the first century.

3. Since the "power of the holy people *[being]* completely shattered" is equivalent to the destruction of Judaism, and since the destruction of Judaism occurred in the first century, that means that the "power of the holy people *[being]* completely shattered" occurred in the first century.

4. The events in Daniel 12:1–2 are among "all these things *[that]* shall be finished" when the "power of the holy people *[had]* been completely shattered."

5. Since the "power of the holy people *[being]* completely shattered" occurred in the first century, and since the events in Daniel 12:1–2 occurred when that power was "completely shattered," that means that the events in Daniel 12:1–2 occurred in the first century.

6. Daniel 12:1–2 are a prophecy about the events of the Second Coming.

7. Matthew 24:31 is a prophecy about the events of the Second Coming.

8. The events of the Second Coming would occur at about the same time, so the prophecy in Daniel 12:1–2 and Matthew 24:31 would occur at about the same time.

9. The events in Daniel 12:1–2 occurred in the first century (see statement #5).

10. Since the events in Daniel 12:1–2 occurred in the first century, and since the prophecy in Daniel 12:1–2 and Matthew 24:31 would occur at about the same time, that means that the events in Matthew 24:31 occurred in the first century.

11. The events in Matthew 24:31 are among "all these things *[that would]* take place" before "this generation *[would]* pass away."

12. Since the events in Matthew 24:31 occurred in the first century, and since the events in Matthew 24:31 would "take place" before "this generation *[would]* pass away," the word "generation" in Matthew 24:34 refers to the first-century "generation" of people.

13. Therefore, in Matthew 24:34, the word "generation" is not referring to "race"; it's referring to the first-century "generation" of people that would "by no means pass away till all these things take place"—which includes the fulfillment of the Second Coming events in Matthew 24:31 in the chart.

The word "generation" in Matthew 24:34 has the same meaning as "generation" in Luke 11:50: they are both referring to the first-century "generation" of people. Luke 11:49–51 was a prophecy about the first-century tribulation of the Jews:

> [49]"Therefore the wisdom of God also said, 'I will send them prophets and apostles, and some of them they will kill and persecute,' [50]that the blood of all the prophets which was shed from the foundation of the world may be required of this generation, [51]from the blood of Abel to the blood of Zechariah who perished between the altar and the temple. Yes, I say to you, it shall be required of this generation."

Thayer defines the Greek word for "generation"—*genea*—in various ways, including "the whole multitude of men living at the same time." Based on our studies in this book, that would be the favored definition for "generation" in Matthew 24:34 and Luke 11:50 above—not "race," as some commentators believe.

* * * * *

Another way to demonstrate that the events of the Second Coming occurred in the first century is by showing the connection between Daniel 12 and Revelation 20 and 21. In the following chart, we'll follow this particular flow of Bible passages:

1. Daniel 12:7 refers back to Daniel 12:1–2.

2. Daniel 12:1–2 is a parallel to Revelation 20:12–13.

3. Revelation 20:12–13 flow into Revelation 21:1, which shows the connection between Daniel 12:7 and Revelation 21:1.

We'll take a closer look at those verses after we look at their flow in the chart on the next page.

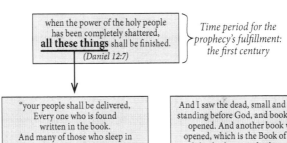

when the power of the holy people
has been completely shattered,
all these things shall be finished.
(Daniel 12:7)

*Time period for the
prophecy's fulfillment:
the first century*

"your people shall be delivered,
Every one who is found
written in the book.
And many of those who sleep in
the dust of the earth shall awake,
Some to everlasting life,
Some to shame and
everlasting contempt."
(Daniel 12:1–2)

=

And I saw the dead, small and great,
standing before God, and books were
opened. And another book was
opened, which is the Book of Life.
And the dead were judged according
to their works, by the things which
were written in the books. The sea gave
up the dead who were in it, and Death
and Hades delivered up the dead who
were in them. And they were judged,
each one according to his works.
(Revelation 20:12–13)

Time period for the fulfillment: still the first century

Then
(Revelation 20:14)

*Time period for the fulfillment:
still the first century*

Death and Hades were cast into the
lake of fire. This is the second death.
And anyone not found written in the
Book of Life was cast into the lake of fire.
(Revelation 20:14–15)

*Time period for the fulfillment:
still the first century*

Now
(Revelation 21:1)

*Time period for the fulfillment:
still the first century*

I saw a new heaven and a new earth, for
the first heaven and the first earth had
passed away. Also there was no more sea.
(Revelation 21:1)

*Time period for the fulfillment:
still the first century*

81

In the chart, the prophecy in Daniel 12:7 said that "when the power of the holy people has been completely shattered, all these things shall be finished." In our study of Daniel 12, we saw that "the power of the holy people" was referring to the first-century Pharisees, scribes, and the other Judaizers, and their power would be "completely shattered" when the great tribulation had ended.

The phrase "all these things" from Daniel 12:7 refers back to Daniel 12:1–2 (indicated by the arrow in the chart), where we see prophecies of some of the Second Coming events: the opening of the Book of Life and the resurrection of the dead for their final judgment.

The chart then shows the parallel between Daniel 12:1–2 and Revelation 20:12–13. Earlier we showed that those two passages were describing the same event, so when Daniel 12:1–2 was fulfilled in the first century, Revelation 20:12–13 was fulfilled then as well. The fact that they were the same event allows the chart to flow from Daniel into Revelation. Daniel 12:1–2 was referring to first-century events, so Revelation 20:12–13—its parallel—was also referring to first-century events. In the chart, as the verses flow from Revelation 20:12–13 into Revelation 21:1, the time period never leaves the first century. In fact, the time connectors "then" (from Revelation 20:14) and "Now" (from Revelation 21:1) show that everything in our chart from Revelation 20:12–13 to Revelation 21:1 would be fulfilled at about the same time.

In our chart, the prophecies in Daniel 12:7 and 12:1–2 occurred at the same time. Since Daniel 12:1–2 flows into Revelation 20:12–13, and since Revelation 20:12–13 flows into Revelation 21:1, that means that the prophecy in Daniel 12:7 (the first verse in our chart) would be fulfilled around the same time as the prophecy in Revelation 21:1 (the last verse in our chart)—and that allows us to create the following logical sequence that shows how the events of the Second Coming were to occur in the first century:

1. Revelation 21:1 and Daniel 12:7 occurred around the same time.

2. Revelation 21:1 was a prophecy about "the first heaven and the first earth *[having]* passed away."

3. We demonstrated earlier that heaven and earth passed away in the first century.

4. Since heaven and earth passed away in the first century, and since the passing away of heaven and earth was a prophecy in Revelation 21:1, that means that the prophecy in Revelation 21:1 was fulfilled in the first century.

5. Since Revelation 21:1 and Daniel 12:7 occurred around the same time, and since the prophecy in Revelation 21:1 was fulfilled in the first century, that means that the prophecy in Daniel 12:7 was fulfilled in the first century.

6. The prophecy in Daniel 12:7 refers back to Daniel 12:1–2 (indicated by the arrow in the chart).

7. Since Daniel 12:7 was fulfilled in the first century, and since Daniel 12:7 refers back to Daniel 12:1–2, that means that Daniel 12:1–2 was fulfilled in the first century.

8. Daniel 12:1–2 are prophecies of some of the Second Coming events: the opening of the Book of Life and the resurrection of the dead for their final judgment.

9. Since Daniel 12:1–2 is a prophecy of the Second Coming, and since Daniel 12:1–2 was fulfilled in the first century, that means that the Second Coming occurred in the first century.

We demonstrated earlier that the passing away of heaven and earth meant that all remaining prophecy had been fulfilled. Since Revelation 21:1 and Daniel 12:7 occurred at about the same time, and since the fulfilled "heaven and earth" prophecy in Revelation 21:1 meant that all remaining prophecy had been fulfilled, that means that Daniel 12:7 was fulfilled at the time when all remaining prophecy was being fulfilled. Since Daniel 12:7 was fulfilled in the first century, that means that all remaining prophecy was being fulfilled in the first century.

There's an additional connection between Daniel 12:7 (the first verse in our chart) and Revelation 21:1 (the last verse in our chart). "*[T]he power of the holy people [being] completely shattered*" from Daniel 12:7 is equivalent to "the first heaven and the first earth *[having]* passed away" from Revelation 21:1. They are referring to the same first-century event: the end of the Mosaic age and the end of Judaism. It was God's destruction of the Levitical priesthood and the sacrificial system by means of the first-century tribulation by the Roman armies. Based on our studies, we can create the following logical sequence:

1. The destruction of Judaism is equivalent to the passing away of heaven and earth.

2. The passing away of heaven and earth occurred at the time when all remaining prophecy was fulfilled, so the destruction of Judaism occurred at the time when all remaining prophecy was fulfilled.

3. The destruction of Judaism occurred in the first century.

4. Since the destruction of Judaism occurred at the time when all remaining prophecy was fulfilled, and since the destruction of Judaism occurred in the first century, that means that all remaining prophecy was fulfilled in the first century.

5. Since all remaining prophecy was fulfilled in the first century, that means that there are no future prophecies yet to be fulfilled.

Earlier in this book, we examined Luke 21:22 and 21:32. In those verses, Jesus was saying that all remaining prophecy would be fulfilled in the first century. We created a table based on those two verses, and we can now add Daniel 12:7 to that table. The verses in that table are paraphrased in the second and third column heads, which say, "In the first century . . . all remaining prophecy will be fulfilled."

Verse	In the first century . . .	all remaining prophecy will be fulfilled.
Luke 21:22	"For these are the days of vengeance,	that all things which are written may be fulfilled."
Luke 21:32	"Assuredly, I say to you, this generation will by no means pass away	till all things take place."
Daniel 12:7	when the power of the holy people has been completely shattered,	all these things shall be finished.

The table shows that in the first century, all remaining prophecy—which includes the Second Coming—would be fulfilled. There are no future prophecies yet to be fulfilled.

Both Luke 21:22 and Daniel 12:7 from the table show the time connection between the great tribulation and the Second Coming. The following chart demonstrates this:

"For these are the days of vengeance, (Luke 21:22)	when the power of the holy people has been completely shattered, (Daniel 12:7)

Both passages refer to the great tribulation of the Jews in the first century.

that all things which are written may be fulfilled." (Luke 21:22)	all these things shall be finished. (Daniel 12:7)

Both passages indicate that all remaining prophecy—which includes the Second Coming—would be fulfilled in the days of the first-century great tribulation.

The following chart shows all the parallels we've identified so far between Daniel 12 and the Olivet Discourse:

"At that time Michael shall stand up, The great prince who stands watch over the sons of your people;" (Daniel 12:1)	"then let those who are in Judea flee to the mountains . . ." (Matthew 24:16–18)	"then let those who are in Judea flee to the mountains . . . (Mark 13:14b–16)

*The protection of the Christians at the time of the
great tribulation of the Jews in the first century*

"And there shall be a time of trouble, Such as never was since there was a nation" (Daniel 12:1)	"For then there will be great tribulation, such as has not been since the beginning of the world" (Matthew 24:21)	"For in those days there will be tribulation, such as has not been since the beginning of the creation" (Mark 13:19)	"For there will be great distress in the land and wrath upon this people." (Luke 21:23)

The great tribulation

"at that time" (Daniel 12:1)	"after the tribulation of those days" (Matthew 24:29)	"But in those days, after that tribulation" (Mark 13:24)

Time period: still the first century in the days of the great tribulation

it shall be for a time, times, and half a time; and when the power of the holy people has been completely shattered, all these things shall be finished. (Daniel 12:7)	"And Jerusalem will be trampled by Gentiles until the times of the Gentiles are fulfilled." (Luke 21:24b)

The last 3½ years of Jerusalem's existence

"when the power of the holy people has been completely shattered . . ." (Daniel 12:7)	"the sun will be darkened, and the moon will not give its light; the stars will fall from heaven, and the powers of the heavens will be shaken." (Matthew 24:29)	"the sun will be darkened, and the moon will not give its light; the stars of heaven will fall, and the powers in the heavens will be shaken." (Mark 13:24–25)

The destruction of the first-century Jewish world—Judaism

". . . all these things shall be finished" ["all these things" are the Second Coming events from Daniel 12:1: the opening of the Book of Life and the resurrection of the dead] (Daniel 12:7)	"and they will see the Son of Man coming on the clouds of heaven with power and great glory. And He will send His angels with a great sound of a trumpet, and they will gather together His elect from the four winds, from one end of heaven to the other." (Matthew 24:30–31)	"Then they will see the Son of Man coming in the clouds with great power and glory. And then He will send His angels, and gather together His elect from the four winds, from the farthest part of earth to the farthest part of heaven." (Mark 13:26–27)

The events of the Second Coming in the first century

The last parallel that we'll examine is the "abomination of desolation" that's mentioned in the Olivet Discourse and Daniel 12:11:

> "Therefore when you see the 'abomination of desolation,' spoken of by Daniel the prophet, standing in the holy place" (whoever reads, let him understand) (Matthew 24:15)

> "So when you see the 'abomination of desolation,' spoken of by Daniel the prophet, standing where it ought not" (let the reader understand) (Mark 13:14)

> "And from the time that the daily sacrifice is taken away, and the abomination of desolation is set up, there shall be one thousand two hundred and ninety days." (Daniel 12:11)

In the Olivet Discourse, Jesus was pointing His disciples to the book of Daniel regarding the "abomination of desolation." This demonstrates that Daniel 12 is directly linked to Matthew 24 and Mark 13, which means that the prophecies in Daniel 12 and the Olivet Discourse—including the prophecy of the Second Coming— were to be fulfilled in the first century.

Let's create a chart that summarizes the connection between Daniel 12 and the Olivet Discourse, and shows how the Second Coming was to occur in the first century.

| "And there shall be a time of trouble, Such as never was since there was a nation, Even to that time." *(Daniel 12:1)* | = | "For then there will be great tribulation, such as has not been since the beginning of the world until this time, no, nor ever shall be." *(Matthew 24:21)* | = | "For in those days there will be tribulation, such as has not been since the beginning of the creation which God created until this time, nor ever shall be." *(Mark 13:19)* |

Time period for the prophecy's fulfillment: the first century

| "at that time" *(Daniel 12:1)* | "after the tribulation of those days" *(Matthew 24:29)* | "But in those days, after that tribulation" *(Mark 13:24)* |

Time period for the fulfillment: still the first century

| "your people shall be delivered, Every one who is found written in the book. And many of those who sleep in the dust of the earth shall awake, Some to everlasting life, Some to shame and everlasting contempt." *(Daniel 12:1–2)* | "they [all the tribes of the earth] will see the Son of Man coming on the clouds of heaven with power and great glory. And He will send His angels with a great sound of a trumpet, and they will gather together His elect from the four winds, from one end of heaven to the other." *(Matthew 24:30–31)* | "Then they will see the Son of Man coming in the clouds with great power and glory. And then He will send His angels, and gather together His elect from the four winds, from the farthest part of earth to the farthest part of heaven." *(Mark 13:26–27)* |

Time period for the fulfillment: still the first century

The Second Coming occurred in the first century because that's when the events of the Second Coming occurred: Jesus coming on the clouds, Jesus sending His angels, the trumpet, the opening of the Book of Life, the gathering (the spiritual harvest/judgment) of God's faithful people, and the resurrection of the dead and their final judgment.

✻ ✻ ✻ ✻ ✻

Earlier in this chapter, we had created a chart that showed how Daniel 12:7 flowed into Revelation 21:1. Before we conclude our study of Daniel 12, let's continue our chart of Revelation by adding Revelation 21:2 and 3. We'll start the chart with Revelation 21:1.

> Now I saw a new heaven and a new earth, for the first heaven and the first earth had passed away. Also there was no more sea.
> (Revelation 21:1)

Time period for the prophecy's fulfillment: the first century

> Then
> (Revelation 21:2)

Time period for the fulfillment: still the first century

> I, John, saw the holy city, New Jerusalem, coming down out of heaven from God, prepared as a bride adorned for her husband. And I heard a loud voice from heaven saying, "Behold, the tabernacle of God is with men, and He will dwell with them, and they shall be His people. God Himself will be with them and be their God.
> (Revelation 21:2-3)

Time period for the fulfillment: still the first century

In Revelation 21:1 in the chart above, we saw that "the first heaven and the first earth had passed away" in the first century, so all prophecy had been fulfilled. God's plan was complete: the righteous were now redeemed, so the fellowship that was lost in Adam was now restored in Christ, symbolized in Revelation 21:2–3 in the chart above. The kingdom had come in its fullness of glory and power, fulfilling the statement that the Hebrew Christians were, at that time, "receiving [present tense] a kingdom which cannot be shaken" (Hebrews 12:28). The arrival of the kingdom in its fullness also fulfilled Paul's statement "that in the dispensation of the fullness of the times He might gather together in one all things in Christ, both which are in heaven and which are on earth—in Him" (Ephesians 1:10).

*   *   *   *   *

Our study of Daniel 12, the Olivet Discourse, and Revelation 20 and 21 showed that the Second Coming occurred in the first century because that's when all remaining prophecy was fulfilled. All of the following events occurred in the first-century days of the great tribulation:

- Jesus coming on the clouds
- Jesus sending His angels
- the trumpet
- the opening of the Book of Life
- the gathering (spiritual harvest/judgment) of God's faithful people
- the resurrection of the dead and their final judgment
- the passing away of the first heaven and the first earth
- the arrival of the new heaven and the new earth
- New Jerusalem descending from heaven

The *timing* of a Biblical event can help determine the *nature* of that event. Since there's no record that Jesus physically came on or in literal clouds in the first century, no trumpet sounded, none of the faithful were physically gathered by the angels, and all of the dead were not physically resurrected, all of those events were not literal; the Bible is using idiomatic language—figures of speech that are common to a particular society, but will be misunderstood by a different society when taken literally. As we mentioned earlier, we'll later examine some of the Second Coming events to see how they are actually figurative and symbolic, and not literal.

In the next chapter, we'll look at some of the Bible's time statements.

Time Statements

We saw how the book of Daniel, the Olivet Discourse, and Revelation prophesied that the Second Coming would occur in the first century. In this section, we'll look at some of the time statements that would have alerted the first-century people to the nearness of the first-century Second Coming.

Earlier in this book, the flowcharts proved that the Second Coming was to occur in the first century. Once something has been proven, it's not necessary to present additional proof. Therefore, the time statements in this chapter are not necessary for proof; however, they support that which has already been proven.

There will likely be some disagreement regarding the interpretation of these time statements. However, the truthfulness of the Second Coming occurring in the first century does not depend on whether we agree on the interpretation of the time statements. For example, if we agree on the interpretation of *all* the time statements, it's a fact that the Second Coming occurred in the first century; if we can't agree on the interpretation of *any* of the time statements, it's *still* a fact that the Second Coming occurred in the first century.

The passages below (under the bold subheads) contain the Greek word *mello*. When we examine the original Greek in each of these passages, we see various forms of that word: *mellei, mellein, mellon, mellontas, mellontes, mellonti, mellonton, mellontos, mellousan,* and *mellouses*. Even though *mello* appears in various forms in these passages, in each instance the word is #3195 in *New Thayer's Greek-English Lexicon*. Thayer defines *mello* in various ways, such as "to be about to do anything," "to be on the point of doing or suffering something," "to intend, have in mind, think to," and "to delay." The fact that the Second Coming was "about to" occur in that first-century generation forces the description of *mello* to be "about to" (or a similar description) in the passages in this chapter.

Most versions of the Bible were created by translators who believed that the Second Coming was still in their future. Since those translators did not believe that the Second Coming was "about to" occur in the first century, they chose not to use the "about to" definition of *mello* in their translations. This book, however, has demonstrated that the Second Coming *did* occur in the first century, so the *mello* passages below, grouped by topic, contain that "about to" definition. As we read those passages, we'll see that God was telling the first-century people that the events of the Second Coming were "about to" occur—in their generation.

Concerning the age about to come (the new heaven and new earth):

"the age <u>about to</u> come" (Matthew 12:32)

not only in this age but also in that which is <u>about to</u> come (Ephesians 1:21)

Let them *[those who are rich]* do good, that they be rich in good works, ready to give, willing to share, storing up for themselves a good foundation for the time <u>about to</u> come (1 Timothy 6:18–19)

the age <u>about to</u> come (Hebrews 6:5)

Concerning the judgment about to come:

"For the Son of Man is <u>about to</u> come in the glory of His Father with His angels, and then He will reward each according to his works. *[Then, to further emphasize the time statement "about to,"* Jesus *said in the next verse,]* Assuredly, I say to you, there are some standing here who shall not taste death till they see the Son of Man coming in His kingdom." (Matthew 16:27–28)

Note: The kingdom is a major topic for study. Regarding the above passage, some Christians believe that the coming of the kingdom occurred on the Day of Pentecost in Acts 2. Actually, Pentecost was when the church began, when believers were added to the church by being baptized into Christ. The coming of the kingdom was one of the events of the Second Coming, when God would redeem the righteous and thus restore the fellowship that was lost in Adam.

Mark 8:38 and the next verse (Mark 9:1), when read together, show how the coming of the kingdom is linked with the Second Coming: "'For whoever is ashamed of Me and My words in this adulterous and sinful generation, of him the Son of Man also will be ashamed when He comes in the glory of His Father with the holy angels.' And He said to them, 'Assuredly, I say to you that there are some standing here who will not taste death till they see the kingdom of God present with power.'"

In Luke's account of the Olivet Discourse, we see in Luke 21:31 that the kingdom of God would arrive after the events of the first-century Second Coming: "So you also, when you see these things happening, know that the kingdom of God is near."

Paul wrote in 2 Timothy 4:1 that Jesus "will judge the living and the dead at His appearing [the Second Coming] *and His kingdom," so the kingdom had not arrived in all its glory on Pentecost. In our study, we saw how Revelation 21:2–3 tell about the coming of the kingdom in its fullness of glory and power, where John "saw the holy city, New Jerusalem, coming down out of heaven from God." This was the spiritual city and Messianic kingdom seen by Isaiah and other prophets.*

He is <u>about to</u> judge the world in righteousness (Acts 17:31)

the judgment <u>about to</u> come (Acts 24:25)

the Lord . . . is <u>about to</u> judge the living and the dead at His appearing and His kingdom (2 Timothy 4:1)

a certain fearful expectation of judgment, and fiery indignation is <u>about to</u> devour the adversaries (Hebrews 10:27)

those who are <u>about to</u> be judged by the law of liberty (James 2:12)

Concerning the salvation/resurrection/glory/life about to come:

there is <u>about to</u> be a resurrection of the dead (Acts 24:15)

[Righteousness] is <u>about to</u> be imputed to us who believe in Him who raised up Jesus our Lord from the dead (Romans 4:24)

having promise of the life that . . . is <u>about to</u> come (1 Timothy 4:8)

those who are <u>about to</u> inherit salvation (Hebrews 1:14)

the glory that is <u>about to</u> be revealed (1 Peter 5:1)

Concerning the world/city about to come:

[the law of Moses is] a shadow of things <u>about to</u> come (Colossians 2:16–17)

Christ came as High Priest of the good things <u>about to</u> come (Hebrews 9:11) the law *[is]* a shadow of the good things <u>about to</u> come (Hebrews 10:1)

[spiritual] city <u>about to</u> come. (Hebrews 13:14)

"Write the things which you have seen, and the things which are, and the things which are <u>about to</u> take place after this" (Revelation 1:19). (*This corresponds perfectly to the earlier words in Revelation 1:1 and 1:3: "things which must shortly take place" and "the time is near."*)

[Jesus] is <u>about to</u> rule all nations (Revelation 12:5)

The above verses contained the Greek word *mello*, and they showed that the events of the Second Coming were "about to" occur in the first century. Let's look at some additional time statements—without *mello*—that would have alerted the first-century people to the nearness of the first-century Second Coming.

"When they persecute you *[Jesus' twelve disciples]* in this city, flee to another. For assuredly, I say to you, you will not have gone through the cities of Israel before the Son of Man comes." (Matthew 10:23)

"And He will send His angels with a great sound of a trumpet, and they will gather together His elect from the four winds, from one end of heaven to the other. . . . Assuredly, I say to you, this generation will by no means pass away till **all these things** *[including that verse 31]* take place *[emphasis added]*." (Matthew 24:31 and 34)

Jesus was indicating that the Second Coming (verse 31) would be one of the events that would occur in that first-century generation (verse 34).

"For these are the days of vengeance *[the first-century days of God's vengeance/tribulation of the Jews]*, that all things which are written may be fulfilled. . . . Assuredly, I say to you, this generation will by no means pass away till all things take place." (Luke 21:22 and 32)

"Most assuredly, I say to you, the hour is coming, and now is, when the dead will hear the voice of the Son of God; and those who hear will live." (John 5:25)

Jesus *[after His resurrection]* said to him *[Peter]*, "If I will that he *[John]* remain till I come, what is that to you? You follow Me." (John 21:22)

And do this, knowing the time, that now it is high time to awake out of sleep; for now our salvation is nearer than when we first believed. The night is far spent, the day is at hand. Therefore let us cast off the works of darkness, and let us put on the armor of light. (Romans 13:11–12)

Let your gentleness be known to all men. The Lord is at hand. (Philippians 4:5)

For this we say to you by the word of the Lord, that we who are alive and remain until the coming of the Lord will by no means precede those who are asleep. (1 Thessalonians 4:15)

For you have need of endurance, so that after you have done the will of God, you may receive the promise: "For yet a *[very, very]* little while *["mikron hoson hoson" in the original Greek]*, and He who is coming will come and will not tarry." (Hebrews 10:36–37)

Therefore be patient, brethren, until the coming of the Lord . . . the coming of the Lord is at hand . . . Behold, the Judge is standing at the door! (James 5:7–9)

[Jesus] is ready to judge the living and the dead . . . the end of all things is at hand. (1 Peter 4:5 and 7)

For the time has come for judgment to begin at the house of God . . . (1 Peter 4:17)

Little children, it is the last hour . . . abide in Him, that when He appears, we may have confidence and not be ashamed before Him at His coming. (1 John 2:18 and 28)

And he *[the angel who showed John the revelation]* said to me *[John]*, "Do not seal the words of the prophecy of this book, for the time is at hand." (Revelation 22:10)

The time statements in this chapter support the first-century timing of the Second Coming. The first-century people were alerted to its nearness, and the Second Coming did indeed occur soon—in that first-century generation.

In the next chapter, we'll examine some of the Bible's figurative and idiomatic language.

Figurative and Idiomatic Language

By using a logical, step-by-step approach to determine the timing of the Second Coming, this book demonstrated that all of the events of the Second Coming have already occurred—in the first century. Since Jesus did not visibly come on clouds, every eye did not literally see Him, the righteous did not physically meet Him in the air, the dead were not physically resurrected, and planet Earth was not literally burned up, that means that those kinds of passages are figurative and symbolic, and not literal. In this chapter, we'll examine some of the Bible's figurative and idiomatic language.

Earlier in this book, the flowcharts proved that the Second Coming was to occur in the first century. As mentioned earlier, once something has been proven, it's not necessary to present additional proof. Therefore, an explanation of the Bible's figurative language is not necessary for proof; however, the explanation of the language supports that which has already been proven.

There will likely be some disagreement regarding the interpretation of these figurative passages. However, the truthfulness of the Second Coming occurring in the first century does not depend on whether we agree on the interpretation of the figurative language. For example, if we agree on the interpretation of *all* the figurative language, it's a fact that the Second Coming occurred in the first century; if we can't agree on the interpretation of *any* of the figurative language, it's *still* a fact that the Second Coming occurred in the first century.

Let's now examine some of the Bible's figurative and idiomatic language.

1

After the resurrected Jesus gave His apostles some final information in Acts 1:1, the Bible tells us the next thing that happened:

> [9]Now when He had spoken these things, while they watched, He was taken up, and a cloud received Him out of their sight. [10]And while they looked steadfastly toward heaven as He went up, behold, two men stood by them in white apparel, [11]who also said, "Men of Galilee, why do you stand gazing up into heaven? This same Jesus, who was taken up from you into heaven, will so come in like manner as you saw Him go into heaven."

Most Christians believe that since Jesus ascended visibly, He would return "in like manner": visibly. However, this book has demonstrated that when Jesus came with the angels in the first century, it was not a visible coming. Therefore, "in like manner" would not be referring to Jesus' visible presence. The phrase "in like manner" was examined by a source that said, "We do not wish for any recognition in its use" (that source didn't want to be credited for its commentary that follows):

> This passage is usually explained as though it read, "as ye have seen him go into heaven, so shall ye see him come again." Those who so interpret the passage explain it as though the point of comparison emphasized in the passage were His being seen going and His being seen coming again, whereas the passage says nothing whatever about His being seen coming again. Hence His being seen coming again cannot be a part of the point of comparison in this passage.
>
> Clearly the point of comparison in this passage is between the manner of His going and the manner of His coming again, and not between His being seen going and His being seen coming again: "This same Jesus . . . shall so come in like manner as ye have seen him go into heaven." Hence this passage treats of the manner of our Lord's Return. And from the manner in which He went we can learn certain things respecting the manner of His Return:

(1) He went secretly so far as the world was concerned, none but His disciples knowing of it at the time; so He comes again secretly ("as a thief in the night") so far as the world is concerned, none but His faithful followers knowing of it in its first stages.

(2) He went away quietly and unostentatiously, without startling the world with a literal trumpet, riding on a literal cloud, shining with a natural dazzling light and blasting the universe into atoms; hence He returns quietly and unostentatiously, without startling the world with a literal trumpet, riding on a literal cloud, shining with a natural dazzling light and blasting the universe into atoms.

(3) He went away blessing those whom He left; hence He returns, blessing first His waiting Church and later the world of mankind.

(4) As respects His Divine body He was invisible to the physical eyes of human beings in His going away, though manifest to His disciples as going by suitable accompanying works; hence on returning He is invisible to the physical eyes of mankind, though He is manifested as present by suitable accompanying works—His works of gathering His elect in the Gospel-Age Harvest, gradually overthrowing Satan's empire in the great Time of Trouble, returning favor to natural Israel, etc.

It's difficult to determine the precise meaning of "in like manner," but since our study of the Second Coming has shown that Jesus did not return visibly and bodily, "in like manner" would not be referring to Jesus' visible, bodily presence. The Second Coming was a spiritual event; Jesus said in Luke 17:20 that "the kingdom of God does not come with observation."

2

In his first letter to the Thessalonians, Paul wrote about the future return of Christ. Paul described one of the events that would happen then:

the future Rapture

> Then *[after the dead in Christ rise]* we who are alive and remain shall be caught up together with them in the clouds to meet the Lord in the air. And thus we shall always be with the Lord. (1 Thessalonians 4:17)

This was one of the events of the Second Coming that occurred in the first century. Since there's no record that the faithful literally rose into the clouds to meet the visible, bodily Jesus, this passage from 1 Thessalonians contains figurative, symbolic language.

The phrase "caught up" comes from the Greek word *harpazo*. Vine says, "This verb conveys the idea of force suddenly exercised." *Harpazo* has various definitions; nonetheless, a figurative interpretation of 1 Thessalonians 4:17 is required since the faithful did not literally rise into the clouds at the first-century Second Coming.

The word "clouds"—when used in connection with the Lord—is associated either with His literal presence (where the "cloud" is literal) or His figurative presence in which His providence (influence) is recognized (where the "cloud" is figurative). Isaiah 19:1 is an example of the figurative, providential presence of God symbolized in a figurative cloud: "Behold, the Lord rides on a swift cloud, and will come into Egypt; the idols of Egypt will totter at His presence, and the heart of Egypt will melt in its midst." The word "clouds" in our 1 Thessalonians 4:17 verse above would also be figurative because in the first-century Second Coming, Jesus did not physically, visibly come in the clouds, and no one physically rose into the clouds.

In the original Biblical text of our 1 Thessalonians verse, there's no "the" before "clouds" or "air." Also, the word "meet" in our verse is actually not a verb in the original text; it's a noun, meaning "a meeting."

The word "air" in that verse is not from the Greek term *ouranos*, which is the term for the space out of our reach (translated as "heavens" nearly every time); it's from *aer*, which is the term for that which surrounds us and which we breathe. Strong seems rather straightforward about this Greek term having reference to where we as humans exist with our own spirit (breath) of life here on planet Earth, not to some space above us in which we can't, as humans, breathe.

Aer or air (that which we breathe, *psucho*) isn't visible and our spirits (*psuche*) aren't visible, thus they exist in that which is invisible. Therefore, when God's kingdom came—being spiritual in nature—it, too, was invisible, without "observation" (Luke 17:20) in both its arrival and its gathering together of God's faithful people.

From this study of 1 Thessalonians 4:17, that verse from Paul would more literally read, "Then we *[I and you Thessalonians]* who are alive and remain will be seized in clouds for a meeting with the Lord in air *[the spiritual realm]*." In other words, there would be a sudden change—"in the twinkling of an eye" (1 Corinthians 15:52)—where the faithful would be given redemption. This sudden change would be unseen; it would occur by faith when the visible promises of A.D. 70 were fulfilled. The very fact that Jerusalem and its temple were destroyed was proof that every other spiritual promise was fulfilled.

3

In the first chapter of Revelation, John wrote about the coming of Christ:

> Behold, He is coming with clouds, and every eye will see Him, even they who pierced Him. And all the tribes of the earth will mourn because of Him. Even so, Amen. (Revelation 1:7)

That verse is parallel to Matthew 24:30:

Behold, He is coming with clouds, and every eye will see Him, even they who pierced Him. And all the tribes of the earth will mourn because of Him. Even so, Amen. *(Revelation 1:7)*	=	"Then the sign of the Son of Man will appear in heaven, and then all the tribes of the earth will mourn, and they will see the Son of Man coming on the clouds of heaven with power and great glory." *(Matthew 24:30)*

In the above verses, the phrases "coming with clouds" and "coming on the clouds of heaven" contain the same symbolism as "the Lord rides on a swift cloud" and "he shall come up like clouds" from the verses below:

Behold, the Lord rides on a swift cloud, and will come into Egypt; the idols of Egypt will totter at His presence, and the heart of Egypt will melt in its midst. *(Isaiah 19:1)*	"Behold, he shall come up like clouds, and his chariots like a whirlwind. His horses are swifter than eagles. Woe to us, for we are plundered!" O Jerusalem, wash your heart from wickedness, that you may be saved. How long shall your evil thoughts lodge within you? *(Jeremiah 4:13–14)*

In those passages from Revelation, Matthew, Isaiah, and Jeremiah, the clouds are not literal; they symbolize the providence (influence) of the Lord who would be "coming" in judgment—via human means, such as armies—to punish His disobedient people. In Revelation and Matthew in chart above, the phrases "coming with clouds" and "coming on the clouds of heaven" are idiomatic expressions that describe the Lord's judgment and destruction of Jerusalem in the first century.

Our study has shown that the events of the Second Coming occurred in the first century, but Jesus did not return visibly and bodily. Therefore, in Revelation 1:7 in the chart above, "every eye" did not see Jesus visibly and bodily "coming with *[literal]* clouds." Likewise, in Matthew 24:30 in that chart, "the tribes of the earth" did not see Jesus visibly and bodily "coming on the *[literal]* clouds of heaven." Instead, when the Jewish nation—"the tribes of the earth"—saw Jesus coming with clouds, and when they saw the sign of the Son of Man in heaven, that means that they saw the *evidence* of Jesus as Jerusalem was being destroyed. They would have recognized, or seen, the hand of God as the architect behind that event. The "tribes of the earth *[would]* mourn" because they had rejected Jesus, and God's vengeance was upon them.

Those first-century people would have "seen" Jesus in the same way that the unfaithful Israelites would have "seen" God when Jerusalem was sacked by the Babylonians in 587 B.C.:

> "Then you shall know that I am the Lord, when their slain are among their idols all around their altars, on every high hill, on all the mountaintops, under every green tree, and under every thick oak, wherever they offered sweet incense to all their idols. So I will stretch out My hand against them and make the land desolate, yes, more desolate than the wilderness toward Diblah, in all their dwelling places. Then they shall know that I am the Lord." (Ezekiel 6:13–14)

Even two thousand years later, we, too, can "see" Jesus in His fulfilled prophecies. When Jerusalem was surrounded by armies, we can see Jesus. When the Christians had fled for safety, we can see Him. When the tribulation occurred—including the destruction of the temple—we can see Him.

Earlier in this book, we demonstrated that the prophecies in Revelation were to be fulfilled in the first century. An additional example is the Revelation verse at the beginning of this #3 section. When we compare it to Zechariah 12:10–14 in the following chart, we can demonstrate that the prophecies in Revelation 1:7 were to be fulfilled in the first century.

Behold, He is coming with clouds, and every eye will see Him, even they who pierced Him. And all the tribes of the earth will mourn because of Him. Even so, Amen. *(Revelation 1:7)*	"And I will pour on the house of David and on the inhabitants of Jerusalem the Spirit of grace and supplication; then they will look on Me whom they pierced. Yes, they will mourn for Him as one mourns for his only son, and grieve for Him as one grieves for a firstborn. In that day there shall be a great mourning in Jerusalem, like the mourning at Hadad Rimmon in the plain of Megiddo. And the land shall mourn, every family by itself: the family of the house of David by itself, and their wives by themselves; the family of the house of Nathan by itself, and their wives by themselves; the family of the house of Levi by itself, and their wives by themselves; the family of Shimei by itself, and their wives by themselves; all the families that remain, every family by itself, and their wives by themselves." *(Zechariah 12:10–14)*

In the chart, we can see that Revelation 1:7 is a reference to Zechariah 12:10–14. That passage from Zechariah is a prophecy about Jerusalem's demise in the first century, so that prophecy from Revelation is also about Jerusalem's destruction.

4

In his second letter, Peter discussed the day of the Lord:

> But the day of the Lord will come as a thief in the night, in which the heavens will pass away with a great noise, and the elements will melt with fervent heat; both the earth and the works that are in it will be burned up. Therefore, since all these things will be dissolved, what manner of persons ought you to be in holy conduct and godliness, looking for and hastening the coming of the day of God, because of which the heavens will be dissolved, being on fire, and the elements will melt with fervent heat? Nevertheless we, according to His promise, look for new heavens and a new earth in which righteousness dwells. (2 Peter 3:10–13)

In the passage above, we see the words "heavens" and "earth." In the Bible, "heavens" and "earth" can refer to the actual heaven and earth, but those words are often used as covenantal language to refer to the covenant between God and man. Let's look at some examples of the covenantal use of "heaven" and "earth."

> [Moses is speaking] "Has He [God] not made you and established you?" . . . [Moses is now quoting God] 'For a fire is kindled in My anger, and shall burn to the lowest hell; it shall consume the earth with her increase, and set on fire the foundations of the mountains.'" (Deuteronomy 32:6b and 22)

In the passage above, God "established" His people through a covenant. Because His people were not faithful, He declared judgment on them through a figurative "fire" that would figuratively "consume the earth." God would punish the "earth" (His covenant people) through His fiery anger; He did not mean that He would literally "consume the *[planet]* earth" with literal fire. Let's look at another example of the covenantal use of "heavens" and "earth."

He shall call to the heavens from above, and to the earth, that He may judge His people: "Gather My saints together to Me, those who have made a covenant with Me by sacrifice." (Psalm 50:4–5)

In the passage above, we see that the concepts of covenant, people, and judgment are connected to the heavens and earth. The Psalmist was using the same kind of figurative language that we saw in the Deuteronomy passage above. Here's another example of the covenantal use of "heavens" and "earth":

"Therefore [because of Babylon's unrighteousness] I [God] will shake the heavens, and the earth will move out of her place, in the wrath of the Lord of hosts and in the day of His fierce anger." (Isaiah 13:13)

The phrases "shake the heavens" and "the earth will move out of her place" are figurative expressions describing God's judgment against Babylon, which was conquered by Cyrus the Great of Persia in 539 B.C. In that verse, God did not literally shake the heavens or literally move planet Earth; instead, that verse is using covenantal language regarding the "heavens" and the "earth." Here's another example from Isaiah:

"And you forget the Lord your Maker, who stretched out the heavens and laid the foundations of the earth. . . . And I have put My words in your mouth; I have covered you with the shadow of My hand, that I may plant the heavens, lay the foundations of the earth, and say to Zion, 'You are My people.'" (Isaiah 51:13a and 16)

The above passages are not referring to the creation of the literal heavens and the literal planet Earth. Instead, those passages are using figurative language, where God's creation of the heavens and the earth is His creation of His covenant with Israel, where He "put My words in your mouth" and called them "My people."

In the 2 Peter 3:10–13 verses at the beginning of this section 4, Peter wrote that the "new heavens and a new earth" would be according to God's promise. The only places in the Old Testament where God promised new heavens and a new earth are found in Isaiah 65 and 66. In Isaiah 65:17-19, after God painted a dismal picture of judgment against Israel, He said,

> "For behold, I create new heavens and a new earth; and the former shall not be remembered or come to mind. But be glad and rejoice forever in what I create; for behold, I create Jerusalem as a rejoicing, and her people a joy. I will rejoice in Jerusalem, and joy in My people; the voice of weeping shall no longer be heard in her, nor the voice of crying."

Like our previous examples, "heavens" and "earth" are used here in a covenantal sense. When God promised to create "new heavens and a new earth," He meant that He would create a new covenant, where "the former *[the Mosaic covenant]* shall not be remembered or come to mind." This was figurative language; God wasn't prophesying that He would create literal new heavens and a literal new planet Earth.

Isaiah 66:22 is the other place in the Old Testament where God promised new heavens and a new earth:

> "For as the new heavens and the new earth *[unlike the old heavens and old earth]* which I will make shall remain before Me," says the Lord, "so shall your descendants and your name remain."

God's prophecy about covenants in Isaiah 65:17 and Isaiah 66:22 is a parallel to Jesus' prophecy about covenants in Matthew 24:35:

"the former [the Mosaic covenant] shall not be remembered or come to mind . . . [but] the new heavens and the new earth [the new covenant] which I will make shall remain before Me" (Isaiah 65:17 and 66:22)	=	"Heaven and earth [the Mosaic covenant] will pass away, but My words [the new covenant] will by no means pass away." (Matthew 24:35)

Note: Jesus' "My words" is referring to the *new* covenant in Matthew 24:35 (above) the same way that God's "My words" is referring to the *old* covenant in Isaiah 51:16 (that we saw earlier).

The following passage—Isaiah 51:6—is an example of figurative language that pictures the passing away of the old covenant and the arrival of the new one in its fullness (when God would grant redemption):

> "Lift up your eyes to the heavens, and look on the earth beneath. For the heavens will vanish away like smoke, the earth will grow old like a garment [the passing away of the Mosaic covenant], and those who dwell in it will die in like manner; but My salvation will be forever, and My righteousness will not be abolished [the arrival of the new covenant in its fullness]."

In 2 Peter 3:10 and 12 (the verses at the beginning of this section 4), we see an additional expression that refers to the passing away of the old covenant: "the elements will melt with fervent heat." We can determine that "elements" is referring to the old covenant because Paul describes those same "elements" in a covenantal sense:

> But now after you have known God, or rather are known by God, how is it that you turn again to the weak and beggarly elements, to which you desire again to be in bondage? You observe days and months and seasons and years. I am afraid for you, lest I have labored for you in vain. (Galatians 4:9–11)

In the above passage, Paul was "afraid for you *[the Galatians]*" because some of them were apostatizing; they were abandoning their faith in Christ by "turn*[ing]* again to the weak and beggarly elements *[the law of Moses]*," where they would "again . . . be in bondage *[instead of in the liberty of Christ]*." They were demonstrating their apostasy by observing the Jewish festivals ("days and months and seasons and years").

Let's now compare the words from Isaiah, Matthew, and Peter to see the parallel covenantal language:

"the former *[the Mosaic covenant]* shall not be remembered or come to mind . . . *[but]* the new heavens and the new earth *[the new covenant]* which I will make shall remain before Me" *(Isaiah 65:17 and 66:22)*	=	"Heaven and earth *[the Mosaic covenant]* will pass away, but My words *[the new covenant]* will by no means pass away." *(Matthew 24:35)*	=	the heavens will pass away with a great noise, and the elements will melt with fervent heat; both the earth and the works that are in it will be burned up . . . all these things will be dissolved . . . the heavens will be dissolved, being on fire, and the elements will melt with fervent heat *[all of those expressions symbolize the passing away of the Mosaic covenant]*. Nevertheless we, according to His promise, look for new heavens and a new earth in which righteousness dwells *[the arrival of the new covenant]*. *(2 Peter 3:10–13)*

Now that we've seen how the passing away of heaven and earth is covenantal language, we can now correctly interpret Revelation 21:1a, which was one of the events of the first-century Second Coming:

> Now I saw a new heaven and a new earth [the new covenant], for the first heaven and the first earth [the Mosaic covenant] had passed away.

As we demonstrated earlier in this book, the passing away of heaven and earth meant that all prophecy had been fulfilled. Since heaven and earth passed away in the first century, there are no future prophecies yet to be fulfilled. God's plan was completed in the first century: the righteous were redeemed, so the fellowship that was lost in Adam was restored in Christ.

Earlier in this book, it was demonstrated that the old heaven and old earth—the Mosaic covenant—passed away after the first-century tribulation. Since the old covenant passed away *after* the tribulation, that means that the old covenant did not end when the law was nailed to the cross (Colossians 2:14). The old covenant would continue until all prophecy had been fulfilled, as Jesus said in Matthew 5:18: "For assuredly, I say to you, till heaven and earth pass away, one jot or one tittle will by no means pass from the law [the old covenant] till all is fulfilled."

When Jesus died, the old covenant was "becoming obsolete" (Hebrews 8:13); it was *not yet* obsolete. In fact, Hebrews 9:9–10 show that God was imposing the Law "until the time of reformation" (when fellowship with God—that had been lost in Adam—would be restored between God and man):

It was symbolic for the present time in which both gifts and sacrifices are offered which cannot make him who performed the service perfect in regard to the conscience—concerned only with foods and drinks, various washings, and fleshly ordinances imposed until the time of reformation.

The old covenant still existed: the temple in Jerusalem still existed, and the Jews who had rejected Jesus were still following the law of Moses with the Levitical priesthood and the sacrificial system. God would bring down Judaism—"what is becoming obsolete and growing old is ready to vanish away" (Hebrews 8:13) and "if what is passing away was glorious, what remains is much more glorious" (2 Corinthians 3:11). Those verses from Hebrews and 2 Corinthians showed that the old covenant still existed after Jesus died (and it still existed after Pentecost in Acts 2).

The old covenant still existed when the book of Hebrews was written. In Hebrews 12:27–28, we see that God would remove "those things that are being shaken" (present tense, referring to the physical things of the old covenant, such as the temple), and those things would be replaced with "a kingdom which cannot be shaken" (the new covenant in its fullness/the New Jerusalem kingdom).

Peter indicated in 2 Peter 3:7 that the old covenant still existed at the time he wrote that second letter, and he wrote that the old covenant would exist until the day of judgment: "But the heavens and the earth *[the Mosaic covenant/Judaism]* which are **now preserved** by the same word, are reserved for fire **until the day of judgment** and perdition of ungodly men" *[emphasis added]*.

God would bring down Judaism, but He wouldn't bring it down until the gospel had been "preached in all the world as a witness to all the nations, and then the end will come" (Matthew 24:14). The phrase "the end" included the end of the old covenant: the destruction of the temple, the sacrificial system, and the Levitical priesthood.

This book also demonstrated that the new heaven and new earth (the new covenant in its fullness) arrived after the first-century tribulation. Since the new covenant arrived in its fullness *after* the tribulation, that means that the new covenant did not arrive in its fullness when the law was nailed to the cross. The faithful did not yet have redemption. That would occur after the first-century tribulation at the arrival of the "new heavens and a new earth *[the new covenant in its fullness]* in which righteousness *[redemption]* dwells" (2 Peter 3:10–13). Here are some examples that show that the new covenant did not begin in its fullness when the law was nailed to the cross:

- In Luke 21:28 (in the Olivet Discourse), Jesus prophesied that redemption—and thus the new covenant in its fullness— would arrive after the events of the first-century tribulation: "Now when these things begin to happen, look up and lift up your heads, because your redemption draws near."

- In Romans 13:11, Paul indicated that salvation—and thus the new covenant in its fullness—had not yet arrived when he wrote that "our salvation is nearer than when we first believed."

- In Ephesians 1:13–14, Paul indicated that redemption—and thus the new covenant in its fullness—had not yet arrived when he wrote that "you were sealed with the Holy Spirit of promise, who is the guarantee of our inheritance until the redemption of the purchased possession, to the praise of His glory."

The old and new covenants are major topics for study. Basically, since the old covenant did not end at the cross, and the new covenant did not begin in its fullness (with redemption) at the cross, there was a transition period when the old and new covenants existed at the same time. The old covenant was approaching its end while the new covenant was approaching its fullness (when God would grant redemption). This transition period is a difficult concept for many Christians, so, in order to understand it, an extensive study is often needed.

The truthfulness of "the first heaven and the first earth" (Revelation 21:1) passing away in the first century does not depend on whether there's agreement on the interpretation of that phrase. For example, if one Christian believes that 1) "the first heaven and the first earth" is referring to the old covenant, 2) the old covenant did not end at the cross, and 3) the new covenant started—but not in its fullness—at the cross, it's a fact that "the first heaven and the first earth" passed away in the first century. If another Christian believes that 1) "the first heaven and the first earth" is not referring to the old covenant, 2) the old covenant ended at the cross, and 3) the new covenant started in its fullness at the cross, it's *still* a fact that "the first heaven and the first earth" passed away in the first century.

Regardless of how a Christian interprets "the first heaven and the first earth," it's still a fact that it passed away in the first century, and because it has passed away, all prophecy has been fulfilled (as we demonstrated earlier).

Let's look at one more example of the Bible's use of figurative language.

5

Revelation 21:1–3, as we examined earlier, pictures the passing away of the old covenant, the arrival of the new covenant in its fullness, and the arrival of the kingdom. Then, in verse 4, John wrote the following:

> And God will wipe away every tear from their eyes; there shall be no more death, nor sorrow, nor crying. There shall be no more pain, for the former things have passed away. (Revelation 21:4)

The source of the above passage is Isaiah 65:19 (its parallel):

> "I will rejoice in Jerusalem, and joy in My people; the voice of weeping shall no longer be heard in her, nor the voice of crying."

This was a prophecy about how God's people would rejoice because the New Covenant (the new heaven and the new earth) would free them from their captivity to sin. God's faithful people would be freed from sin when they received redemption at the Second Coming. Let's read again that verse from Isaiah, but we'll also read the two verses preceding it to see how God's creation of the new heavens and a new earth (the New Covenant in its fullness with redemption) would produce joy in His faithful people:

> "For behold, I create new heavens and a new earth; and the former shall not be remembered or come to mind. But be glad and rejoice forever in what I create; for behold, I create Jerusalem as a rejoicing, and her people a joy. I will rejoice in Jerusalem, and joy in My people; the voice of weeping shall no longer be heard in her, nor the voice of crying." (Isaiah 65:17–19)

Revelation 7:14–17 pictured this same promise to the faithful who came through the great tribulation of the first century:

"These are the ones who come out of the great tribulation, and washed their robes and made them white in the blood of the Lamb. Therefore they are before the throne of God, and serve Him day and night in His temple. And He who sits on the throne will dwell among them. They shall neither hunger anymore nor thirst anymore; the sun shall not strike them, nor any heat; for the Lamb who is in the midst of the throne will shepherd them and lead them to living fountains of waters. And God will wipe away every tear from their eyes."

By saying that hunger, thirst, discomfort, and sorrows would be removed is not meant that the church would never again experience persecution. The above passages from Revelation and Isaiah are simply using figures of speech that describe how the redeemed would have no more sorrow over being sin-laden.

* * * * *

In the next chapter, we'll identify some reasons why most Christians firmly believe the traditional view of the Second Coming.

The Firm Belief of the Traditional View

Most Christians firmly believe that the Second Coming is a future event. They believe that Jesus will return literally and bodily. Here are some reasons why this traditional view is generally accepted:

- Most Christians haven't studied the Second Coming in the kind of detail presented in this book. They haven't seen flowcharts that demonstrate how the events of the Second Coming occurred in the first century. They also haven't seen a study of the time statements or the idiomatic language.

- I know from my own personal experience that when we've been taught something repeatedly for many years, that teaching becomes truth to us. The longer we're exposed to that teaching, the more deeply rooted it becomes. It often gets to the point where we'll believe our teaching cannot contain error. We'll embrace that teaching so firmly that we'll believe it cannot be wrong. We'll be reluctant to listen to a different viewpoint—even if that different viewpoint happens to be correct.

That same situation occurs when a Christian is repeatedly exposed to the traditional view of the Second Coming. He'll be taught about the future return of Christ in sermons, prayers, and songs such as "Jesus Is Coming Soon," "We'll Work Till Jesus Comes," and "When the Roll Is Called Up Yonder." The longer this Christian is exposed to the traditional view, the more deeply rooted it becomes. He'll get to the point where he'll believe it's impossible for the traditional view to be wrong. He'll embrace that view so firmly that he'll be reluctant to listen to a different view—even if that different view happens to be correct.

- Most Christians believe that the events of the Second Coming are literal because they *sound* literal. The Bible contains accounts of many miraculous events, so at the Second Coming, it's conceivable that Jesus could come bodily with the angels, the dead could be physically resurrected, the faithful could literally rise to meet Jesus in the air, and planet Earth could be burned up.

- Most Christians support the traditional view because they take literally today what wasn't taken literally in that Jewish culture 2,000 years ago on the other side of the planet. We admit that we have idioms, such as "spill the beans" and "you're pulling my leg," that wouldn't be understood in an Asian culture if those idioms were taken literally; likewise, we should admit that the Bible has idioms we won't recognize if we take them literally.

Those were some reasons why most Christians firmly believe in the traditional view of the Second Coming. Let's look at some problems that can occur when we believe a Bible issue too firmly.

Potential Problems from a Firm Belief

When a Christian develops a view about a future Second Coming, he needs to be careful. He can get to the point where he believes his view cannot be wrong. When he gets to the point where he believes it's impossible to be in error, he won't want to listen to another viewpoint—even if that other viewpoint happens to be correct.

A person can firmly believe that he has a correct interpretation of a particular Bible subject, but his interpretation could still be wrong. For example, one person might believe that salvation occurs at baptism, while another person believes that salvation does *not* occur at baptism, but instead he believes it occurs when a person puts his faith in God and Jesus by believing that God exists and that the Bible is God's word. Each of those two people has been exposed to his particular doctrine for many years, and each one can refer to specific Bible passages to try to prove his viewpoint. Each of them firmly believes his particular view about salvation, but both views cannot be correct because they're opposites regarding baptism. One of those people is wrong regarding baptism, even though that person firmly believes his particular viewpoint.

That demonstrates how a person can firmly believe in his interpretation of a particular Bible subject, but his interpretation can still be wrong. Even Paul firmly believed that he was doing the right thing by persecuting Christians before he was converted and saw God's truth. A person can have a firm belief, but even a conviction can be wrong if it's not based on the Scriptures. A Christian can firmly believe that the Second Coming is a future event, but that firm belief is still wrong.

Reviewing Our Study

This book presented charts, tables, and logical sequences that demonstrated how the Second Coming and the fulfillment of all remaining prophecy occurred in the first-century days of the great tribulation of the Jews. That first-century timing was the basis for some logical conclusions:

- The fact that the Second Coming was "about to" occur in that first-century generation forces the description of *mello* to be "about to" (or a similar description) in the passages in the "Time Statements" chapter.

- The fact that the Second Coming occurred in the first century forces a figurative, idiomatic interpretation to most of the events of the Second Coming, including passages of Jesus coming on clouds, the rising of the faithful to meet Jesus in the air, the resurrection of the dead, and the passing away of the first heaven and the first earth.

- The fact that the Second Coming occurred in the first century means that the passing away of the first heaven and the first earth—one of the events of Second Coming—also occurred in the first century. Our study demonstrated that the passing away of heaven and earth occurred at the time when all remaining prophecy was fulfilled. Since the passing away of heaven and earth occurred at the time when all remaining prophecy was fulfilled, and since the passing away of heaven and earth occurred in the first century, that means that all remaining prophecy was fulfilled in the first century. There are no future prophecies yet to be fulfilled.

Based on our studies in this book, we can create the following logical sequence:

1. The Second Coming was to occur in the days of the great tribulation.

2. The great tribulation occurred in the first century.

3. Since the Second Coming was to occur in the days of the great tribulation, and since the great tribulation occurred in the first century, that means that the Second Coming occurred in the first century.

4. Since there's no record that Jesus and the angels visibly appeared at the Second Coming, that means that the Second Coming was a spiritual, non-visible event.

Some people who believe that the return of Jesus was to be visible and bodily also believe that the Second Coming was to occur in the first century. Since Jesus did not return physically in the first century, those people don't have faith in the Bible; they don't believe that Jesus kept His promise about a first-century return, so they don't believe that He's the Messiah. If those people were to read this type of book, they might reconsider their viewpoint and see that Jesus really did return in the first century, and that He really is the Messiah—and then they might seriously consider becoming Christians.

Most Christians have been raised in the traditional view that the Second Coming is a future event and that Jesus will return literally and bodily. That belief is usually so deeply rooted that it's difficult to change that belief. However, we should admit to ourselves that it's possible for our viewpoint to be wrong, so if someone wants to share a different view, we should be willing to listen.

We should strive to be open-minded like the Bereans in Acts 17:11–12. When Paul and Silas preached the Word to them, the Bereans didn't immediately accept the message, nor did they immediately reject it; they took the time to study the message by "search*[ing]* the Scriptures daily to find out whether these things were so." God commended them for being "more fair-minded than those in Thessalonica." They were open-minded enough to consider whether they might have been wrong.

From those two verses in Acts, we can learn three things about what it means to be truly opened-minded in God's sight:

- Open-minded people give those with a differing belief a fair and honest hearing. (In John 7:51, Nicodemus asked the Pharisees, "Does our law judge a man before it hears him and knows what he is doing?")

- Open-minded people weigh the beliefs and evidence presented by others in the light of the Scriptures.

- Open-minded people willingly admit when they've been wrong and make the necessary changes.

In His parable about the man who sowed seed, Jesus said that some of the seed "fell on good ground and yielded a crop: some a hundredfold, some sixty, some thirty" (Matthew 13:8). Later, when He explained the parable to His disciples, the Lord told what He meant by "good ground":

- In Luke's account, He characterized the "good ground" as those who have a "noble and good heart" (8:15).

- In Matthew's account, He characterized the "good ground" as one who "hears *[listens to]* the word and understands it" (13:23).

- In Mark's account, He characterized the "good ground" as those who "accept" God's Word (4:20).

Putting it all together, we have this: an open-minded person is one who has a good and honest heart that listens to, understands, and accept God's Word.

As we study the Scriptures, our understanding can be aided by external sources such as commentators and historians. However, those sources are not the actual Scriptures, so external sources are not inspired and thus can contain error. Whenever there's a contradiction between an external source and the Bible's internal evidence, the latter should be favored.

Most Christians hopefully have a great love for the Bible, and they genuinely want to understand God's word. We'll become skillful interpreters when we're able to distinguish the figurative language from the literal language. Our interpretation of the Second Coming will contain error when we interpret literally the passages that were meant to be figurative—which is the error that most Christians have made regarding Jesus coming on clouds, the rising of the faithful to meet Jesus in the air, the resurrection of the dead, and the passing away of the first heaven and the first earth. When we read the Bible, we should put ourselves in the shoes of the original audience—generally composed of Jews—so that we can try to understand the Scriptures the way God intended them to be understood.

Misinterpretation of the Scriptures has caused division among Christians. In 1 Corinthians 1:10, Paul instructed his brethren to "all speak the same thing, and that there be no divisions among you, but that you be perfectly joined together in the same mind and in the same judgment." We can avoid divisions and be "perfectly joined together" when we allow the Bible to interpret the Bible, being careful not to read anything into the Scriptures to force them to fit our personal viewpoint.

When we understand that all prophecy has been fulfilled, our faith can actually grow. For example, when we understand that Revelation was describing first-century events, our confidence in the truthfulness of the Scriptures will increase. In Revelation, we'll see that God accurately foretold the events leading up to A.D. 70. A person who doesn't believe in the Bible might convert to Christianity when he recognizes God's awesome ability to foretell those first-century events.

If a person reads this book but still believes that the Second Coming is a future event where Jesus will return bodily and the dead will physically rise from their graves, that person might consider creating a series of charts, tables, and logical sequences—as this book did—to demonstrate his futurist belief.

* * * * *

The Bible is the most important book ever written. We should all strive for a clear understanding of God's Word. The better we understand the Bible, the better we know God.

Living Righteously

If we believe that God existed in Bible times—and therefore exists today—we'll want to obey His commands.

In the Old Testament, Psalm 111:10 says,

> The fear *[great admiration and respect]* of the Lord is the beginning of wisdom; a good understanding have all those who do His commandments. His praise endures forever.

The New Testament continues that teaching. Mark 12:28–31 contains an account of a scribe (an expert and teacher of the Jewish Law) who asked Jesus,

> "Which is the first *[principal or most important]* commandment of all?"

> Jesus answered him, "The first of all the commandments is: 'Hear, O Israel, the Lord our God, the Lord is one. And you shall love the Lord your God with all your heart, with all your soul, with all your mind, and with all your strength.' This is the first commandment. And the second, like it, is this: 'You shall love your neighbor as yourself.' There is no other commandment greater than these."

We demonstrate our love for God by genuinely trying to obey Him at all times. In 1 John 5:3, it says, "For this is the love of God, that we keep His commandments. And His commandments are not burdensome." Our obedience to God should be our top priority; it should come before everything else in our lives.

The Bible guides us into becoming the kind of people that God desires. We could make the world a better place if we all tried to follow Jesus' teaching in Luke 6:31 and Paul's teaching in Romans 13:8–10:

> "And just as you want men to do to you, you also do to them likewise."

> Owe no one anything except to love one another, for he who loves another has fulfilled the law. For the commandments, "You shall not commit adultery," "You shall not murder," "You shall not steal," "You shall not bear false witness," "You shall not covet," and if there is any other commandment, are all summed up in this saying, namely, "You shall love your neighbor as yourself." Love does no harm to a neighbor; therefore love is the fulfillment of the law.

Hebrews 11:6 says,

> But without faith it is impossible to please Him, for he who comes to God must believe that He is, and that He is a rewarder of those who diligently seek Him.

Having faith in God and Jesus means that we'll believe that God exists and that the Bible is God's word. We'll trust in God and His Son, and we'll try to obey the Bible's commands for righteous living. When we "diligently seek Him" and put our faith in Him, we'll trust that we'll be rewarded with eternal life—we'll continue to live in God's presence after our physical lives have ended (leaving unbelievers without that reward).

46515070R00078

Made in the USA
Lexington, KY
06 November 2015